Small Group Learning in the Classroom

Jo-Anne Reid, Peter Forrestal and Jonathan Cook

HEINEMANN
Portsmouth, New Hampshire

IRWIN PUBLISHING
Toronto, Canada

HEINEMANN EDUCATIONAL BOOKS, INC.
361 Hanover Street
Portsmouth, NH 03801
Offices and agents throughout the world

Published simultaneously in Canada by
IRWIN PUBLISHING
1800 Steeles Avenue West
Concord, ONT L4K 2P3

This edition first published in North America in 1990 simultaneously by Heinemann and Irwin Publishing. This edition first published in Australia in 1989 by Chalkface Press and the Primary English Teachers Association. An earlier edition, titled *Small Group Work in the Classroom*, first published in Australia by the Education Department of Western Australia.

Library of Congress Cataloging-in-Publication Data
Reid, Jo-Anne, 1952-
    Small group learning in the classroom/Jo-Anne Reid, Peter Forrestal, and Jonathan Cook.
      p. cm.
    Reprint. Originally published: Chalkface Press, 1989.
    Includes bibliographical references.
    ISBN 0-435-08542-5
    1. Learning. 2. Group work in education. 3. Classroom environment. 4. Interaction analysis in education. I. Forrestal, Peter, 1944- . II. Cook, Jonathan, 1944- . III. Title.
LB1060.R4 1990
371.3′95 – dc20
                          90-35956
                            CIP

Canadian Cataloguing in Publication Data
Reid, Jo-Anne, 1952-
    Small group learning in the classroom

Includes bibliographical references.
ISBN 0-7725-1817-3

1. Learning. 2. Group work in education. 3. Classroom environment. 4. Interaction analysis in education. I. Forrestal, Peter, 1944- . II. Cook, Jonathan, 1944- . III. Title.
LB1060.R45 1990   371.3′95   C90-095105-2

Designed by Stephen Mellor
Edited by Bronwyn Mellor and Jeremy Steele
Illustrated by Sharon Thompson, Jo-Ann Reid and Janis Nedela
Typeset in New Century Schoolbook by Lamb Printers P/L, Perth, Australia

Printed in the United States of America
10 9 8 7 6 5 4 3 2 1

Contents

For Garth Boomer

Acknowledgements

The first edition of this book had its origins in the work of the Language and Learning Project, 1977-82 (Western Australian Education Department), the Geraldton Project, 1978-79 (Schools Commission), and the Kewdale Project, 1981 (Education Department of Western Australia and the English Teachers Association of Western Australia). We acknowledge the major contribution to these projects and this book of Bill Louden and Bill Green.

We also acknowledge the valuable contribution of Barrie Hepworth (Teacher Development Branch of the Western Australian Education Department, 1979 - 81) and Peter Renshaw to this book.

Our work has been significantly influenced by our interaction with friends and colleagues from overseas, in particular Alan Howe and the Wiltshire Oracy Project, John Johnson and the National Oracy Project (UK), Ann Shreeve and Sandra Howard of the Norfolk Oracy Project and Mark Brubacher of the York Board of Education, Toronto.

We are extremely grateful to Jeremy Steele for his rigorous and thoughtful editing and the members of the PETA Board for their valued comments on the manuscript.

We thank Christine Cook and students of Melville Senior High School, Barbara Davidson and students of Subiaco Primary School, Gary Davidson, Tom McHenry and students of Hamilton Hill Senior High School, Gill Swan, Shane Negus and students of John XXIII College and Pam Woodcock and students of Claremont Primary School.

Note:
- involvement in the task
- security of the friendship group
- confidence of the learners.

1 Learning

Psychologists tell us that humans are naturally inquiring animals. We have an innate need to make sense of the world we inhabit - a need to make meaning - that remains with us all our lives. From earliest childhood, humans assume the task of learning about the world, about themselves and about each other. The first and prime means that we use for this lifelong process of discovery is our language, for it is through thinking, interaction and co-operation with other people that our capacity and potential for learning increases and develops. Indeed our individual understandings and ways of thinking arise from, and are formed by, our cultural and social interactions.

The learning that takes place in our daily lives is, therefore, predominantly **social**: it arises from our need to solve problems that involve other people, or to imitate the skills we see other people using; from our natural exploration and play in the world; from the guidance or the requirements other people present to us; and from the sheer emotional pleasure that we take from our interactions with significant people in our lives. It is only through these social uses of language, initiating each of us into the culture of our society, that children are enabled to use language to explore the world individually.

These 'natural' learning processes are, to a large extent, the same processes that teachers attempt to recreate in classrooms in order to teach children the things that societies deem necessary for a useful and rewarding existence. But classrooms are structured and contained social environments, with their own institutionalised relationships of power and behaviour. The interactions that take place in them are often based more on institutional needs than on our understandings of human learning.

Indeed, the arrangement of thirty or so children compelled to spend up to six hours a day with one adult in one room can be seen as a rather 'unnatural' social situation, which creates its own patterns of behaviour and interaction that have to be **learned** by students when they enter school, if they are ever to learn other things in this situation. Often, and quite necessarily, behavioural learnings about living in classrooms take priority over the more explicit curricular offerings of the school - with the result that a great deal of time in class seems to be taken up with students learning how to adapt to the classroom culture, rather than learning the content of the curriculum.

Thus the human tendency for learning is often not aligned with the requirements of the school situation. What the teacher is required to teach children may not be the same as what children want, or need, to learn. And so the teacher must find ways of using the social situation within the classroom to best advantage - turning it from something which needs to be contained and managed to conform to a single institutional framework, into a rich and fruitful context in which students can and will learn - naturally.

Learning and Language

Language not only describes the world, it also plays a part in shaping the way we see it. Our theory of learning has developed from a consideration of the earliest attempts of children to make sense of their world - through the use of language.

From infancy, we use language in order to regulate, order, classify and offer explanation for the world we see around us; and to communicate our needs, requests, problems and thoughts to our fellows. The child's use of language provides the potential for continuing to grow and develop as a human being. By the time children start school, they are already expert at using language to function in the world, and have a rich resource base that teachers can use for further learning.

Language helps us make sense of the world. The classroom, therefore, should be a place where language flows freely and readily from and between the people who are there to learn - the students. The classroom where students are using their language to come to terms with new information, to make sense of it so that it can become their own, is the context in which the most effective learning will take place.

For students to learn to use their own thinking and language to help them learn, the classroom should be a place where their language and ideas are valued, and are seen to be valued. This is why the idea of the **small group** of students as the basic unit of classroom organization is both useful and practical, as well as being theoretically sound. The classroom which thus asserts the value of social and collaborative interaction as fundamental to human learning is one where students are able to learn most easily - using their expertise in making sense of the world and its ideas.

Learning in the Classroom

It is a basic tenet of this book that, for good learning, the classroom is best organised on a collaborative basis.

Teachers cannot simply transmit information to their students and assume that it will be learned. For students to understand new information, they must be given the opportunity to engage in the processes of **coming to know** - through problem solving, exploration, observation and practice - with direction and assistance from the teacher. They must become actively involved with the information they are attempting to learn, in ways that are most conducive for learning.

This means that the teacher, aware of the types and variety of thinking and talk possible in the classroom, is constantly striving to raise the levels of student thinking about, and interaction with, new content material.

Levels of thinking

A hierarchy of levels of thinking, closely following the work of James Moffett, demonstrates the range of levels of thinking and language available to students and teachers in the classroom:

theorise	high levels of thinking
speculate / hypothesise	
generalise	
report	
record	low levels of thinking

A simple **record** of information (notes from the board, transcription of ideas or observations of phenomena or events) gives little opportunity for students to engage, though it might be a useful basis for further thinking and transformation.

Tasks that require learners to **report** such recorded information to others (most simply to a partner or other members of a small group) require a deeper engagement with the information, ideas, and meaning. This is because the changes in language required for reporting make demands on the learner.

Similarly, tasks requiring the individual or small group to **generalise** from reported instances involve students directly in reformulating and rethinking prior experience and language towards this more demanding end.

When students are required to **speculate** or **hypothesise**, predicting possible results, reasons, events, phenomena or attitudes on the basis of their records, reports or generalisations, they must literally rethink their earlier experience and understanding even further.

And at the highest level, questions such as *What if?* encourage the learner to synthesise and connect existing knowledge and understandings in such a way as to **theorise** about potential possibilities and problems - or, in Jerome Bruner's sense, to move well beyond the information given.

It seems obvious that higher level thinking tasks, by their nature more interesting and rewarding than simple recording and reporting, are key factors in the degree to which students will become more involved and more active learners.

Intending to learn

Students will learn best if their **intention** to learn is aroused. Within the classroom, this is most likely to occur if they:

• have a clear sense of direction and purpose

• can build upon what they already know

• are actively participating, using their own language and cultural images to help them understand.

Students are most likely to become actively involved in the learning activities taking place in the classroom if they:

• have a supportive environment - one that provides a healthy degree of tension, yet allows them to feel free to make mistakes

• have a degree of choice and responsibility for what, when and how they learn

• have time to think and reflect about what they have learned

• have time to explore how they learn.

Learning theory

Learning can be seen as a process that extends, in some way, the existing views of the world which individuals have. It adds to their life experience, by altering or building on the meanings that they have made of the world and the way it works.

The learning that takes place in classrooms can be depicted in the following manner: the learners, and their life experiences, interact with new information to create a larger experience which forms the basis for future learning. The type and quality of the interaction between the individual and the new information will depend to a large extent upon the view of learning, or the learning theory, on which the teacher has based the classroom structure and organisation.

The ideas and suggestions in this book are based on a learning theory that takes into account the innate human desire to make sense of the world - a desire that differs in degree and depth as children develop. The theory also assumes that much of the learning that happens in school takes place in classrooms - particular social sites with their own rules and conventions of behaviour and interaction - where teachers' knowledge about how children learn will influence both the quality and quantity of learning for any group of students.

Advantages of Learning in Small Groups

Allowing students to work in small groups gives them a greater share in the classroom's talk space and should contribute to their language development.

It is easier to listen carefully as a member of a group of four rather than as a member of a class of thirty. The greater intimacy and involvement which the small group offers, together with the greater opportunity to respond to and act on what others say, make it a better situation for developing students' listening abilities than a whole class discussion.

Best use of the learning time

Small groups enable students to make the best use of the learning time in the classroom.

- Students generate more ideas in collaborative settings than they do individually or in a whole class group.

- Students have more incidental and planned opportunities to use language (reading, writing, listening, talking) as an instrument of learning.

- Students can learn from each other and they can teach each other, explaining, questioning, reminding and imagining, in the language and patterns of interaction with which they are most practised and comfortable.

- Students can learn to recognise that their own experience and thoughts are of value when they are learning new information.

A co-operative learning environment

The classroom organised around the basic unit of the small group will produce a co-operative learning environment that supports students' efforts.

- Students develop confidence in themselves as learners.

- Students who are quiet in the more formal classroom setting will talk.

- Students will be prepared to think aloud as they use talk in an exploratory way to wrestle with new information, or to make sense of new experience.

- Students will generate tentative suggestions and half-formed ideas that will help themselves and the group move closer to understanding.

- Students will gain confidence in presenting findings to a critical audience because they have the opportunity to sort the ideas out first.

- Students will develop their sense of audience and appropriateness of both oral and written language for different purposes.

- Students will develop an awareness of the differences between **exploratory** talk or writing, preparation, practice or rehearsal, and written or oral **performance**.

A beneficial teacher-student relationship

The classroom organized around the basic unit of the small group will also produce a beneficial teacher-student relationship.

- The role of the teacher changes from that of the person who imparts knowledge to that of the person who is responsible for carefully structuring the learning experiences and assisting students in their learning.

- The teacher can listen carefully to small group discussion, monitor student talk to gauge the level of understanding, and provide assistance when necessary (often immediately).

- The teacher has time for personal contact. When the class is working in small groups, the teacher is free to deal with individuals in a way that is not possible when handling the class as a whole group.

Flexibility of classroom organisation

Three kinds of groups are referred to in this book: **Home Groups** (the working groups in which students normally operate, or the groups in which they begin the particular lesson or unit of work), **Sharing Groups** (into which students are directed to make public the results of their work) and the **Whole Class**.

The classroom organised around the basic unit of the small group allows for great flexibility of classroom organisation.

- Students in Home Groups can easily work individually or in pairs; can move to form a wide range of reconstituted Sharing Groups, or operate as a Whole Class. The determining factor is the form of organisation most suited to the particular learning activity.

- Students can seek information according to their needs at any particular time, and can seek it in the way that suits them best - from the teacher, from text or reference books, from other students or from other resources.

Not only does the Home Group provide a secure and supportive base from which the students can venture out and return as they need, but it also provides a manageable and flexible base from which the teacher can work to provide the best learning experiences for the individual students within the class.

As teachers become more familiar with and proficient in organising, managing and planning for small group learning (in all primary and secondary years and in all subject areas), they will find that what may, at first, seem to be a complicated and apparently major shift in their own professional learning, is, in fact, merely a means of enabling them to use their existing knowledge and expertise more efficiently.

The small group is the basic unit of classroom management.

2 Learning in the Classroom

This chapter suggests a framework or model through which students can move **from information towards understanding**. All modes of language (reading, writing, listening and speaking) are involved in, and central to, each stage of the learning process on which the model is based.

If teachers want students to understand what they teach, they must give them the opportunity to personalise knowledge. Teachers cannot give students knowledge; they can only help them come to know by providing structures within which students can develop their own understandings.

The model of learning below can apply to single lessons, to work lasting for a couple of lessons, or to whole units of work. It is essentially a programming guide that enables teachers to plan for a class to work in small groups in such a way that learning can best take place.

It is the task of the teacher to structure the work of the classroom so that significant learning, which generally involves time, effort and a measure of struggle, will occur. This framework suggests that learning involves a process and one way to describe that process is to consider that it consists of the following five stages.

Engagement: teacher provides input to whole class.

Exploration: small group exploratory talk.

Transformation: students engage in an activity to reshape information.

Presentation: pairs combine to share results of activities.

Reflection: Whole Class discusses the learning process after small group reflection.

A Model of Learning

Engagement

The Engagement Stage is the time during which students acquire information and engage in an experience that provides the basis for, or content of, their ensuing learning. It should involve a shared experience for students so that they have common ground on which to base their learning. Input may be provided in a wide range of ways, including:

- teacher talk
- reading - stories, poetry, reference books, textbooks, newspapers or magazines
- film, television, or other visual means
- radio, tape recordings, records
- blackboard explanations
- demonstrations
- excursions.

On some occasions, this stage will have as its beginning point a sharing of the students' knowledge and experience. This is a useful strategy to focus their attention on the topic and engage them in its study.

This initial stage of the learning process should involve more than the teacher providing students with new content material. For the students to become engaged in an activity, they need to understand **why** they are examining this particular topic, text, information or material. They also need to understand how this particular lesson, or unit of work, fits in with what they have done before and what they will study in the future.

Learners need not only a sense of direction but also a sense that they **are** learning - that is, that there has been a change, a growth, and a development in their understanding of the world and their place in it. This is something that teachers have to prepare and plan for, explicitly and deliberately. It should never be a case of teacher and students simply growing old together.

Students generally become engaged, or their **intention** to learn is aroused, when they become curious or puzzled about what they are to learn. They need to recognise the problematic and want to solve their puzzlement. It must, therefore, matter to them as well as to their teacher.

By the end of the Engagement Stage, students need to have the territory they are to explore charted and to have a clear sense of the required outcomes. Further, they should be conscious of ways in which their learning path is going to reach these outcomes. Clearly, the teacher has responsibility for providing their direction but, ideally, the more the students contribute the better.

Teacher action

Engagement

- encourages reflection

- reviews progress so far

- points to further directions

- poses organising questions

- encourages prediction and hypothesising

- presents new content material

- links new material with old

- provides structured overview

- demonstrates or models new skills

most often used

least often used

Engagement

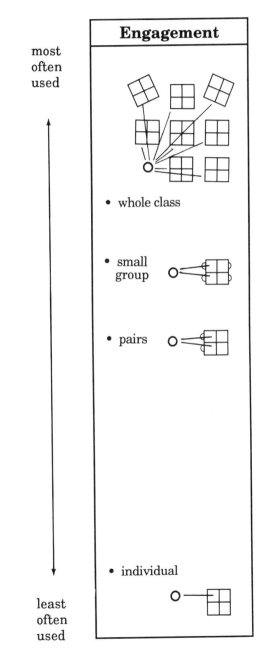

- whole class

- small group

- pairs

- individual

Exploration

At this stage of the learning process, students have the opportunity to make an initial exploration of the new information. They can make tentative judgements as they bring their past experience and understandings to bear, and they are free to make mistakes or not fully understand.

Exploration should encourage thinking aloud and so, in most cases, it is best achieved if students work in Home Groups of four. However, there will be times when exploratory talk will be more successful in pairs, and other times when individual exploratory writing will be more appropriate.

The focus at this stage is not on language being used to communicate what is known, but on language being used as an instrument of learning. Thinking aloud, for example, enables students to use talk to grapple with ideas and to clarify thoughts. It is a time during which students are likely to be hesitant and tentative.

This is a vital stage in the learning process, and time and opportunity should be provided for it as a regular part of the **teaching** routine. In other words, this apparently unstructured time must be built into the structure of the learning process.

Whenever students encounter new information, they need to have the chance to explore it for themselves first, before being asked to engage with it in particular ways. So there must be a gap between the Engagement Stage and the Transformation Stage during which no task is set by the teacher.

Although exploratory talk may occur at all stages of the learning process, the Exploration Stage is different from the others in that it is the time when teachers deliberately take a step back and remove themselves from the classroom discourse. They become observers, monitoring students' activity - watching, listening, and learning just how much (or how little) information and experience the learners are bringing to the task.

In addition, the emerging enthusiasms, puzzlements and questions, the background information students have, the difficulties they are finding in making connections between their prior experience and the new material - all become available to the teacher who is carefully monitoring exploratory activity, so that adaptation or revision of the planned activity in the Transformation Stage is possible.

Teachers also need to monitor the amount of time students have for exploration - making adjustments so that they have neither too much nor too little time for profitable discussion. In a typical lesson, this might involve a period of between three and ten minutes.

Teacher action

Exploration

- facilitates development of group skills

- provides time for students to make their own links with the information

- may provide time for individual writing for this purpose

- may provide direction through open-ended questioning

- monitors small group talk closely - does not contribute

- reflects on information gained from monitoring student talk

most
often
used

least
often
used

Exploration

- small group

- pairs

- individual (exploratory writing)

Transformation

Students continue to operate in Home Groups during this stage of the learning process, with the teacher intervening and explicitly asking the students to use or to work with information in order to move towards a closer understanding of it. They are asked to focus their attention on the aspect (or aspects) of the information which leads to the desired outcomes of the learning activity.

Transformation activities might involve clarification, ordering, reorganising, elaborating, practising or using the information in a purposeful way.

The choice of activities will be determined by the aims of the teacher's programme and will be crucial to the results and quality of student learning. Any text or piece of information is susceptible to a wide range of possible transformations, all of which could involve learners in potentially profitable activity, but only some of which will lead students towards an understanding of the material most appropriate to a particular teaching context.

For example, one activity which can help students understand a particularly complex story is drawing a picture of it. This requires them to examine the story closely in order to decide on the best way to represent it pictorially. A transformation activity such as this is unlikely to be particularly appropriate with a story which is straightforward and does not require detailed examination.

In working on a particular activity, the group should have a clear idea of the amount of time they have to complete their task and the anticipated outcomes. They should also know how they are expected to present their findings.

The teacher's role during this stage is partly to monitor the students' learning and partly to teach. Teachers are most likely to teach on a one-to-one or small group basis in response to student needs. They have to be constantly roving and available to intervene:

- to correct misconceptions

- to provide additional information

- to guide students in the development of their learning

- to reset short-term objectives.

Teacher action

Transformation

- recalls directions

- sets Transformation activities

- organises classroom appropriately

- reviews constraints

- facilitates development of writing, reading and speaking skills, as appropriate

- directs students to best resource material

- monitors students' progress and understanding

- monitors quality of work produced

- provides new information where necessary (by recycling the Engagement and Exploration Stages)

- records progress of students

most
often
used

least
often
used

Transformation

- small group

- pairs

- individual

Presentation

Students are asked to present their findings to an interested and critical audience in their Sharing Groups. Requiring students to explain what they have learned can play a worthwhile part in the process of moving from information towards understanding. It provides a degree of tension and gives a sense of purpose to the work of the Home Groups. Having to explain what they have learned to an interested group reinforces their understanding of new information and, in fact, often enables them to test for themselves whether they really know what they are presenting. In addition, the feedback students receive enables them to determine how successful their work has been.

Reporting the findings of the Transformation Stage to the whole class should be a rare occurrence. The size of the Whole Class group and the potentially repetitive nature of reporting back impose severe limitations on its use.

It is preferable for the findings of Home Groups to be made public within Sharing Groups, which may be formed by combining:

- one representative from each of four different Home Groups
- two students from one Home Group with two from another
- two students from three different Home Groups
- two Home Groups of four.

Teachers' decisions on the grouping for the Presentation Stage will depend on the task and the teaching point which they wish to make. In many cases, teachers may use the rearrangement of groups to achieve other goals, such as mixing groups of boys with girls or less capable students with more able ones.

During the Presentation Stage, teachers have the opportunity to check whether students have learned what was intended and to monitor what else they have come to understand through the process. Thus, Presentation can be a three-fold stage: it shows what has been learned; it exposes what is still uncertain; and it reveals what is still to be learned. From here, it's on to Reflection and closure; or back to Exploration and Transformation. And if there is a need for further teacher input - it's back to Engagement and the model is worked through again.

This is the most appropriate stage for assessment, as students are asked to use language to communicate what they have learned. It is a time for clear, precise communication.

Teacher action

Presentation

- provides sense of
  performance by
  explicitly valuing
  the work produced

- ensures products have
  been shaped to suit
  given audience and
  purpose

- organises classroom
  appropriately

- encourages audience
  response and feedback

- encourages sharing of
  products

- facilitates development
  of presentation skills,
  such as:

  - handwriting
  - layout and design
  - editing/proofing
  - rehearsal
  - public speaking
  - oral reading

- evaluates products
  of students in terms
  of goals (where
  necessary)

most
often
used

least
often
used

Presentation

- larger groups

- reconstituted
  small groups

- small groups
  combine

- whole class

- wider audience

- individual to
  small group

Reflection

Reflection plays an invaluable part in learning. By looking back at what they have learned and the process they have gone through, students can gain a deeper understanding of both the content and the learning process itself. This should help them with their future learning and should increase their sense of involvement in, and control of, the learning process.

Learning should involve an individual and collaborative Reflection Stage, in order to fix the learning and to make some sense of it in its entirety.

The kind of questions students should ask themselves include:

• What have I learned?

• How do I feel about this?

• How important is it to me?

• How does this connect with what I've learned before?

• Have I done what I set out to do?

• What do I need to learn next?

• What did I think of the learning process?

• In what ways can I improve my own learning?

Asking students to reflect upon what and how they have learned also helps the teacher to monitor the learning programme, and to plan further activities.

Of course, reflection on the process can and should occur at the Exploration and Transformation Stages and reflection on the products of the learning at the Presentation Stage. By focussing attention on and indicating the value of reflection, teachers can encourage the development of a working atmosphere in the classroom - as students take increasing responsibility for their own learning.

Teacher action

Reflection

- reviews products and outcomes of learning

- reviews the learning process

- shows enthusiasm and disappointment

- encourages students to evaluate their own progress in terms of curriculum aims

- organises classroom appropriately for:

  - individual writing
  - small group talk
  - whole class discussion

- re-establishes links between this activity and whole curriculum

- solicits student ideas on follow-up activities, future directions and extension work

- reflects upon all this for future planning

most
often
used

least
often
used

Reflection

- small groups

- pairs

- individual

- whole class discussion

A Summary of the Model of Learning

Engagement

The Engagement Stage is the time during which students acquire information and engage in an experience that provides the basis for, or content of, their ensuing learning. It should involve a shared experience for students so that they have common ground on which to base their learning.

Exploration

This is a vital stage in the learning process, and time and opportunity should be provided for it as a regular part of the **teaching** routine. Though apparently unstructured, it must be built into the structure of the learning process. Whenever students encounter new information, they need to have the chance to explore it for themselves first, before being asked to engage with it in particular ways. In other words, there needs to be a gap between the Engagement Stage and the Transformation Stage during which no task is set by the teacher.

Transformation

Transformation activities require students to focus their attention on the aspect (or aspects) of the information which represent the desired outcomes of the learning activity. Students continue to operate in Home Groups during this stage, with the teacher intervening and explicitly asking the students to use or to work with information in order to move towards a closer understanding of it.

Presentation

Students are asked to present their findings to an interested and critical audience in their Sharing Groups. Requiring students to explain what they have learned can play a worthwhile part in the process of moving from information towards understanding. It provides a degree of tension and gives a sense of purpose to the work of the Home Groups. Having to explain what they have learned reinforces students' understanding and often enables them to test for themselves whether they really know what they are presenting. In addition, the feedback they receive enables them to determine how successful their work has been.

Reflection

Reflection plays an invaluable part in learning. By looking back at what they have learned and the process they have gone through, students can gain a deeper understanding of both the content and the learning process itself. This should help them with their future learning and increase their sense of involvement in the **learning** process.

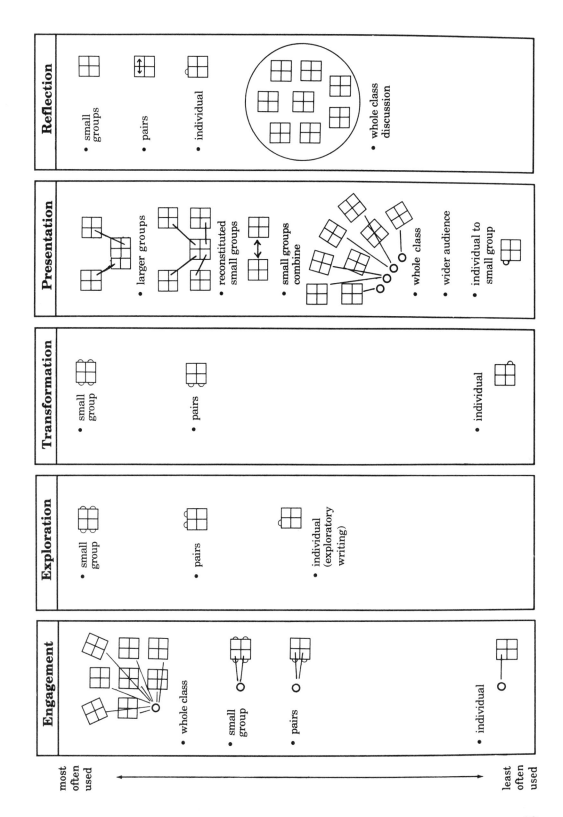

Reflection
- small groups
- pairs
- individual
- whole class discussion

Presentation
- larger groups
- reconstituted small groups
- small groups combine
- whole class
- wider audience
- individual to small group

Transformation
- small group
- pairs
- individual

Exploration
- small group
- pairs
- individual (exploratory writing)

Engagement
- whole class
- small group
- pairs
- individual

most often used ←——————————→ least often used

29

Small Groups - the Basic Unit of Classroom Organisation

With this framework for planning, the small group will be seen as the basic unit of classroom organisation. Of course, at different times, the students will be working in a variety of ways: individually, in pairs, in their Home Groups, in Sharing Groups or as part of the Whole Class. Just how they operate at each stage of the learning process will be determined by the teacher, depending on the nature of the task, the needs of the learners, and the aims and intended outcomes of the lesson or unit of work.

Home Groups may also be the best environment for solitary activity such as reading or writing. This is unlikely to be true if groups lack direction and purpose (when gossip and chatter will inevitably prevail) or if they are unused to working in the ways outlined in this book. But when groups are set purposeful tasks, when students are aware of the potential of the small group for powerful learning and when they are familiar with this approach, even the very youngest will accept that there are times when silence, concentration and non-talk activity are important.

When students see small groups as the central unit of classroom organisation, they come to regard small group discussion and sharing as an important and normal part of the learning process. They move smoothly into and away from small group talk - as well as to and from individual reading or writing and listening to the teacher.

Start in Home Groups

It is recommended that Home Groups be structured by the students on the basis of friendship and that Sharing Groups be structured by the teacher depending on the aims and intended outcomes of the lesson.

It's best for students to work in friendship groups of four during the Exploration Stage because, in this arrangement, they feel most secure. The emphasis during Exploration is on allowing students to think aloud and formulate tentative hypotheses, and they are more at ease among their friends than in structured interest or ability groups.

It may not be possible, or appropriate, to form friendship groups in the junior primary years, particularly at the start of Year 1. Teacher-organised Home Groups, structured according to age (for instance), have proved to be effective at this time.

Groups of four students are recommended for two reasons:

- All students can be seated facing each other, yet no student need have her or his back to the board or to the teacher when the teacher is at the front of the room.

- Four seems to be the optimum number that allows for a good range of experience in the group, as well as for individual contributions. Within larger groups, the contributions of quieter members may be overlooked.

During the Transformation Stage, teachers can decide whether to allow the groups previously set up to continue to work together, or whether to structure groups according to other criteria. Because of the dynamic interaction that develops fairly quickly when a small group of students is working together purposefully, the teacher is able to take into account the individual differences and needs of students when making a decision whether or not to regroup.

Move to Sharing Groups

During the Presentation Stage, the teacher's role in influencing the composition of groups should increase as other considerations, such as the following, become important.

- In a mixed-sex class, there may be value in asking a group of boys to combine with a group of girls at this stage - both from a sociological point of view and because it may create a little more constructive tension in the groups as they communicate their ideas.

- A group that appears to be having difficulty can often be combined with a group which has found the task easier, so that this stage can also serve as a consolidation of learning for the latter group. This setting encourages fruitful peer-tutoring.

- Groups presenting their work or ideas to larger audiences, or to audiences outside the classroom, will feel an increasing responsibility to work toward a quality product.

Back to Home Groups

At the Reflection Stage, friendship groups again provide the security that allows students to draw on their past experiences and relate them to new information. Extended small group discussion helps students to understand their friends' attitudes and values, and thus leads to a deeper understanding.

Conditions for Purposeful Talk

Purposeful small group talk is likely to occur when:

- the classroom atmosphere encourages co-operative learning
- students have an appropriate amount of time to complete their activities
- they are required to make their findings public.

Classroom atmosphere

While classroom atmosphere is something that develops over the year, it is important that from the outset teachers show by the physical organisation of the classroom, and by their own words and actions, that small group talk is a valuable part of the learning process.

Students must feel that they have a worthwhile contribution to make, and that their own language is a valuable learning tool. The teacher, aware of this, should value the often vague and tentative language used by students while they are coming to know.

As their understandings develop, students should move towards more explicit 'public' language to articulate what they know. Technical or subject-specific language can become part of a learner's working vocabulary only if its meaning is understood.

Working with small groups can also help teachers to overcome some of the problems they face when dealing with a whole class, such as talking too much, making all the decisions for students, or questioning inefficiently.

Time

The question of time is a vital one for successful small group learning. If students do not have enough time, they cannot engage in the necessary exploration. If they are under too much pressure, they are unlikely to learn effectively. When students feel they do not have enough time, and are worried about completing the task in the set period, the working of the small group may suffer.

However, if students have too much time to complete a task, they are likely to waste it. In the early stages particularly, clear tasks to be done in a comparatively short time are best. Teachers and students will learn to use and allocate time more efficiently as they become more experienced in small group work.

Striking a balance between the extremes of giving too much or too little time for completing tasks is one of the most difficult issues that teachers face when managing small groups, and there's no easy answer. The teacher needs to know his or her students and to monitor carefully what is happening as the groups progress through the various stages of the learning process.

Generally, however, it is a question of time being reorganised. It may well be that students need more time in the earlier stages of the learning process, but do not need as much time in the later stages. For example, students who have spent time exploring and talking about a new problem in mathematics will find that they need less time to practise different examples of the problem, because their understanding has developed at the earlier stage.

Making the findings public

The quality of discussion at the Transformation Stage is improved when students know that they are required to make public the findings of their group. However, this does not mean that groups should spend time reporting to the class, as this is often both unnecessary and inefficient. It should only happen when there is genuine expectation in the class to hear from a student or group, and then only when groups have not all been discussing the same question.

There are better ways of achieving the purposes of reporting back, including these.

• Requiring one representative from each of four Home Groups to form a Sharing Group to pool their results and check their understandings.

• Asking each of four Home Groups to examine different aspects of the topic or to examine the subject matter from different angles. Sharing Groups, made up of one representative from each of those four groups, are then formed to share the information gathered.

• Requiring each Home Group to put their findings on a blackboard, or a large sheet of paper, for other class members to examine critically.

• Asking each student to explain what the Home Group has come up with to the person sitting in the matching position in the next group.

• On some occasions, larger Sharing Groups may be appropriate. Groups of eight can be formed by asking two Home Groups to compare notes, by asking pairs from four groups to combine, or by asking one student from each of eight Home Groups to work as a Sharing Group. Similarly, groups of six can be formed in a variety of ways.

Reconstituting Small Groups

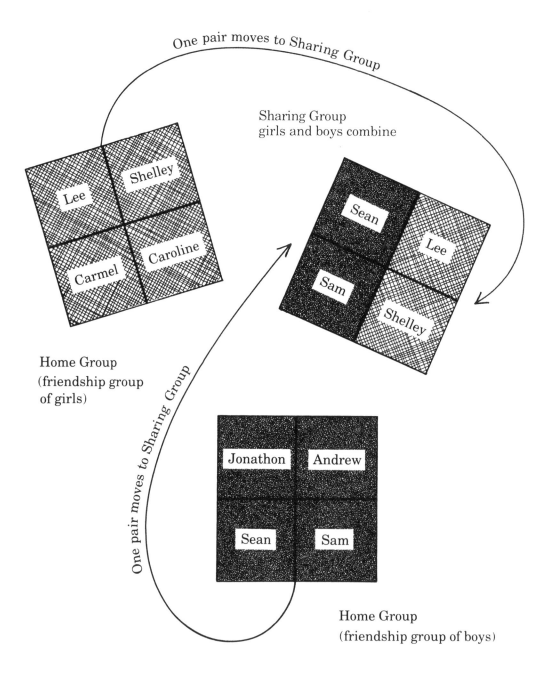

One pair moves to Sharing Group

Sharing Group
girls and boys combine

Lee

Shelley

Carmel

Caroline

Sean

Lee

Sam

Shelley

Home Group
(friendship group
of girls)

One pair moves to Sharing Group

Jonathon

Andrew

Sean

Sam

Home Group
(friendship group of boys)

Home Group to Sharing Group

(Science topic Year 6 - Insects and how they move)

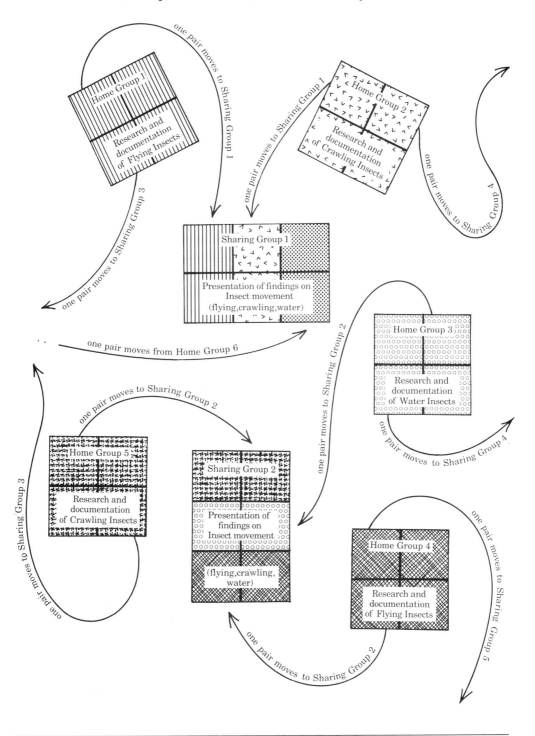

Note:
- involvement of group can be seen in interactive body language such as leaning forward, good eye contact
- everyone is required to take notes

- students working alone, pair writing on the computer
- teacher provides instruction at the point of need.

3 Managing Small Groups

Students will work effectively in small groups when they believe that their work has a purpose and when the small group structure is appropriate to the task. **Simply arranging the classroom furniture into groups will not result in effective group work.** Like adults, students like to talk, and a group of students sitting together will generally do just that. But the kind of talk that takes place, and its quality, will depend upon the students' perceptions and acceptance of the purpose of their talking together. This chapter outlines some of the requirements that teacher and students must meet to make small groups work effectively.

Talk should not be seen by students as an end in itself, or a chance to do nothing in class. When small group work is first being implemented, students, particularly older ones, may think that they are doing nothing when they are working in small groups.

Historically, talking has been seen as a punishable offence in schools, so the teacher who encourages students to sit together in small groups of friends and talk may be seen by them as having no 'real' work planned, an ulterior motive or a headache.

Teachers need to show that they value student talk

Of course, it may not be easy to convince some students that the instruction to **talk about** new information is worthy of their careful attention and thought. But students realise very quickly, if it is pointed out to them, that their talk does in fact help them to understand better. Therefore, teachers who value student talk need to say that they do. And they need to prove that they do by allowing students to stop and talk among themselves about, say, questions asked of the whole class, a difficult word met in a text book, or a sample mathematical problem on the blackboard.

Teachers who stop to give students five minutes to clarify what has been said have little trouble convincing them that talk is valuable. This will be so especially if they explain why they are encouraging talk at this time, or if they give the students an opportunity to reflect on how the talking has helped to clarify their thinking. Similarly, the teacher who thinks aloud for the class when trying to explain something, who makes a tentative guess at the result of a problem or the meaning of a word, explaining the reasoning behind the guess, has little trouble convincing students that they, too, might offer tentative thoughts and ideas to the small group.

Students need to prepare for small group discussion

If students are given the opportunity to think or write for themselves for a few moments before the small group discussion begins, they are forced to focus on the task at hand. This pre-talk activity is likely to be non-threatening as students are making personal notes to jog their memories - rather than communicating with a critical audience.

Obviously this is not a strategy for every occasion but, used thoughtfully, it can be extremely useful for focusing the talk. Making exploratory notes before a discussion ensures that all group members have thought about the topic beforehand and have something to contribute. For younger children, the teacher will need to model and demonstrate the use of **key words** rather than fuller notes, so that almost from the time they start school, young learners are attempting to use writing and reading as an aid to their thinking and talk.

Group leaders should not be appointed

Although there may be times when a group leader or reporter is required, these occasions should be rare and, even then, the reporter should be appointed by the group rather than the teacher. Many teachers have noticed unsuccessful group work after they have appointed a leader because the other group members felt little responsibility for the results of their work.

A group of four does not need a leader to chair discussions. If the students are working together to grapple with new information or working on a clearly defined task, different students will adopt the leadership role at different times, and the resulting sense of group identity is much stronger than it is in groups that operate with an appointed leader.

The other functions of group leaders (such as recording the group's findings on a large piece of paper or reporting to the whole class) can be shared among group members, thus giving each student the opportunity to practise the skills involved.

Everyone in the group is required to take notes

If one student in the group is appointed recorder, there is a tendency for the others to sit back and hand over responsibility for the the group's efforts to that person.

Even when the group is recording their findings for public appraisal, each student should feel responsible for taking notes as an aid to learning. Students need to realise that taking notes can help them understand new information better, and therefore most of the time, especially during the Exploration and Transformation Stages, **all** students should be note-takers.

Once students have become used to this approach to small group work, they will accept that taking notes and keeping their own records are natural parts of the learning process. And, of course, they will readily appreciate that when Sharing Groups are formed by one member from four different Home Groups combining, it becomes essential for each individual to have notes on the findings of their group.

Students need to understand group processes

Groups of four students facing each other in a self-contained unit will easily discover how its dynamics differ from those within groups larger, smaller or otherwise arranged physically. It is important to alert students to the effects of distance, body language, size and familiarity on the functioning of different groupings.

The suggested approach to 'Getting Started' (outlined in Chapter Five) is one way of alerting students to this important aspect of small group work. Students need to be aware of the group as an entity; of the necessity for members to work together and contribute to the group; and of the effect of dominating individuals on the group's functioning.

An understanding of the processes of small group work is best developed through experience and practice, but the teacher needs to create an initial awareness of them and to build upon it during the Reflection Stage.

Chapter Seven points out the need for teachers to plan for this type of learning about group processes from the beginning of every new year, and to nurture the development of students' understandings through careful and explicit attention to them throughout the year.

Students need to have clear and appropriate tasks

The tasks set for small group work should be appropriate both for the students' abilities and interests and for the aims of the teaching programme.

Students need to know the desired outcomes of each group activity so that they are able to judge the effectiveness of their discussion and their product. If there is no clarity of purpose, the learners will have little chance of achieving the outcomes of the unit of work.

This does not mean that the teacher should foreshadow the results of a particular discussion, but that the task must be clearly established. There seems little value in arranging small group discussion with the bare direction, 'Discuss'. The learners need to know the purpose of the discussion - for example, whether it is to clarify the information presented, or to look at the content from a different point of view, or to rank the three most significant features in order. Simple directions may be enough, but they must be given.

Students must be free to work alone when necessary

There are many times when students may need or want to work as individuals. They must be free to leave the group, either physically or mentally, as the requirements of the task dictate.

Individual note taking, thinking, writing and reflection are essentially private activities which have to be catered for. Maintaining silence while the whole class is working individually, or providing quiet areas within the room, may be appropriate strategies.

The illustration below shows how this can be organised. Students who wish to work alone, or students who are required to work alone, for either discipline or control reasons, are easily accommodated within this framework.

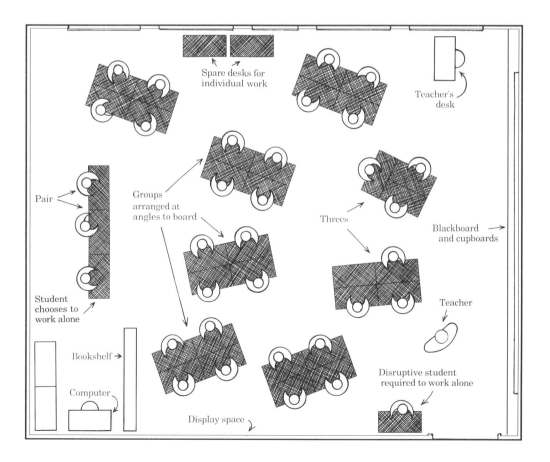

The teacher can provide help without dominating.

Note:
- teacher helps individual while the others continue their own work
- teacher positioning is collaborative, not dominant
- body language and concentration of group members
- small group work gives teacher opportunities to deal with individuals without holding up the rest of the class

- teacher interacts with Home Group.

4 The Role of the Teacher

Teachers who are unused to operating along the lines suggested in this book are likely to find that, when they adopt the approach it advocates, their role in the classroom undergoes a significant change. Traditionally, teachers make most of the decisions in their classrooms and little time is allocated to discussion in small groups. Most discussions involve the whole class and are controlled by the teacher, who does most of the talking, asks almost all the questions, and evaluates most replies.

For teachers who have reservations about making the small group the basic unit of classroom organisation, the sections which deal with whole class discussion and questioning (pp. 52-55) offer advice about giving students greater opportunities for thinking within the traditional classroom. This advice may provide a useful bridge between present practice and an eventual move to the regular use of small groups.

The purpose of this chapter is to help teachers become more confident in managing small groups, and to provide practical guidelines for classroom planning and methodology.

Planning for Small Group Learning

One of the keys to successful small group learning is careful planning by the teacher - a topic further explored in Chapter Seven. The learning experience should be structured so that students have the opportunity to build on what they already know, have a clear sense of direction, have enough time to develop their understandings, and are required to make their findings public in some way.

Students must be given the opportunity to explore new ideas, to grapple with them and to make these ideas their own. The stages of learning (described in Chapter Two) provide a framework for teachers to achieve this.

When programming, teachers can use this book's model of learning to ensure that their planning is as effective as possible. The following questions provide a checklist for planning and preparation.

At the Engagement Stage

- Are my goals clear?
  Do I know exactly what I want the students to learn?

- Are my students aware of the goals and desired outcomes?

- Are students encouraged to ask questions about what they are learning and why they are learning it?

- Is the information I have prepared clearly expressed, well organised, and easy to comprehend?
  Is it logical?
  Can they read it?
  Are new or difficult terms introduced?
  Is it presented in the best possible way?
  Do I need diagrams, a film or other illustrations?

- Have I provided suitable resources?

- Have I provided enough information or made sure that the shared experience will provide enough?
  Is there too much information for the students to absorb?

- Have I developed a logical sequence for the understandings involved?

Unforeseen diversions, interruptions or surprise events can be incorporated into the work of the classroom if the teacher allows for them when planning.

At the Exploration Stage

- Have I allowed an appropriate amount of time?

- Do the students know what is expected of them?

- Can I monitor the groups as they work to see how the students process the information and how it fits in with their past experience and present understandings?

- Can I take note of misconceptions or misunderstandings that arise and adapt future input or transformation activities to overcome these?

- Am I able to keep out of exploratory discussion unless I am questioned or asked for clarification?

It is often difficult to accept that students engaged in exploration are keeping to the task. Because of the tentative nature of exploratory talk, students often seem to be digressing from the point as they use their personal life experiences to make sense of the new. The teacher should be aware of this and understand that it is a valuable part of learning - which will pay dividends as the learning process continues.

At the Transformation Stage

- Can I continue to monitor the work of the small groups so as to provide any additional information required by one group, a number of groups, or the whole class?

- Can I deal quickly with any misconceptions or questions from individuals or groups, or refer them immediately to other resources for clarification?

- Have I prepared additional information which may be useful as resource material for those students who need extending?

- Are the tasks set at this stage designed to lead the students towards achieving the goals I have set?

- How can I take into account the differing ability levels of the students? Are the tasks I have set suitable?

Although it is important to take account of the difficulties that may confront students who are less able at, or less interested in, a particular task, it must be remembered that small group work often provides the support and sharing that less able students need to achieve more success. The threat of failure for these students is also less acute when they are working in a context that encourages them to seek help from their friends.

At the Presentation Stage

- Have I made sure that the students are aware of their audience and its particular requirements? (For example, teaching a new mathematics problem to another class in the same year means that the language and form of the presentation used can be similar to those of the students' own classroom experience. Teaching it to a class of younger students, however, will make different demands.)

- Have I made clear to the students the way in which their work will be assessed? Or have I negotiated with them about this? If the work is to be presented to an audience beyond the classroom, who should assess it?

- What factors will influence the decisions I make about the kind of Sharing Groups that must be organised at this stage? For example, will I ask a pair from one group to combine with a pair from another group to give students the security of working with one of their Home Group? Or will I ask one student from each of four Home Groups to form a Sharing Group so as to create a degree of tension and ensure that they all prepare adequate notes while working in their Home Groups?

- What other considerations should affect the structure of the Sharing Groups? For example, will I ask pairs of girls to combine with pairs of boys? Will I ensure that each group has a mix of abilities? If I am moving a pair from a Home Group, will I allow students who are sitting together to move or will I choose those sitting opposite or diagonally opposite each other?

- If the presentation is to take the form of a written document, have I made sure that all group members have their own copies?

- Is the material presented at this stage sufficient to show that the students have accomplished the goals of the learning experience? Is anything else required of them or me?

During the Presentation Stage, the teacher has the opportunity to make certain that the students have learned what was intended. The fact that they have done the work does not necessarily mean that they have learned. The teacher can also evaluate what the students have come to understand about the process.

At the Reflection Stage

- Have I encouraged students to reflect on the process of learning as well as on what they have learned?

- Do their reflections attempt to evaluate the goals of the learning experience?

- Can I use their reflections as a means of assessing the effectiveness of my programme or as a basis for future planning?

The reflection that takes place during or after any learning is particularly important for the learners, as it allows them to place a value on the work that has been done, as well as to consider the manner in which the learning has taken place. For students to become independent learners, it is essential that they become aware of how they learn. Time for reflection and discussion with peers allows for this.

Operating Small Groups

Organising classrooms so that students work in groups of four is a skill to be developed through experience. The more confident and experienced a teacher becomes, the more effective students' work in small groups is likely to be.

Teachers and students need to see small group work as an important learning activity. Therefore it should be part of everyday classroom routine. In addition, students need to realise that talk helps their learning and can indeed be hard work.

In the classroom where the small group is the basic unit of classroom management, the role of the teacher alters substantially. However, the teacher still needs traditional teaching skills such as:

- carefully preparing and structuring the learning experience

- setting goals or helping students to set goals

- providing information or helping students to find information

- helping with resources

- setting reasonable deadlines

- being available for consultation, and being a good listener

- directly teaching individuals, groups or the whole class when necessary

- being aware of what's happening at all stages during the lesson

- providing an orderly and well-disciplined classroom.

Successful learning in small groups is most likely to occur in a classroom that is well organised and controlled. Such an environment is not at odds with relaxed and friendly relations between students and teacher. When students are treated with respect and have some control over the pace and direction of their learning, their power to learn in small groups is unleashed.

Monitoring student learning

Teachers can learn a great deal about the individual student's involvement in small group discussion by simply standing back and observing what is happening in each group.

In the early exploratory stages the teacher should monitor talk unobtrusively. Students need time to explore and assimilate new information and the teacher should intrude as little as possible. It's not always necessary to hear every word of a discussion to know what is going on. Indeed it's possible to monitor by listening to the tone of the talk, by watching the faces of the students, and so on. It's also often possible to listen to a discussion while looking in another direction, or to gauge the degree of involvement within a group while moving past it.

As the students move beyond the exploratory stage, the teacher should continue to monitor the discussion carefully, tracing the students' developing understanding and giving help when it is asked for. There will be times when the teacher will correct misunderstandings that have arisen in discussion, although it should be remembered that the process is designed to enable students to correct such misunderstandings themselves.

For example, asking two groups to compare their ideas encourages them to clarify their thinking before they start talking to each other. The act of explaining helps clarify it further and provides an opportunity for the students to correct each other. If teachers listen carefully during the Presentation Stage, they can gain a clear understanding of how well students have understood or solved a given problem.

When a teacher overhears a misunderstanding or a misconception in one or two groups, it is difficult to resist the temptation to call the whole class together. Although this may be necessary sometimes, it is often much better to overcome the problem by helping students in their groups. Before stopping the whole class to give an explanation, the teacher needs to be reasonably certain the problem is one that requires such an interruption.

There obviously will be times when the teacher has to interrupt a small group of students for reasons of discipline - for example, when the group has wandered off the task or is wasting time.

A further reason for careful monitoring of groups is that the teacher needs to check whether students have enough time to complete their tasks and whether they are ready to move on to the next stage.

Body language and small group work

The teacher should be aware of the effect that an outsider has on a group's functioning and should take this into account whenever interrupting a group. Body language is particularly important here, as the messages the body conveys can often work against the teacher's best intentions.

The illustrations below depict three ways in which the teacher can interact with a working group. In the first, the teacher is standing and has positioned himself outside the group space.

Any conversation that is directed to the group from this position will result in the students either stopping what they are doing to listen or, if they are involved in the task at hand, missing the teacher's instruction, request or question.

The teacher in the second illustration has moved into the group space physically, enabling the students to regard the intrusion as part of the functioning of the group, rather than as an interruption imposed from the outside. The teacher, by watching and listening for an opportune time to interrupt, will be sure of gaining the attention of the whole group.

In the third illustration the teacher has again become part of the group and, by positioning himself so that he has close physical and eye contact with the group, is able to interpose suggestions, directions or information as an intrinsic part of the group process. This type of teacher positioning is also best for talking with an individual student while the rest of the group continues to work.

Classroom furniture

The activity in which students are engaged should determine the arrangement of classroom furniture. For instance, desks can be arranged to clear a space for students to construct a model or set up a scientific experiment, and sometimes a performance space may be desirable at the Presentation Stage.

When a full class discussion is to take place, the furniture should be arranged so that all students can see each other. A circle seems the ideal pattern. One variation that may provide a useful practical alternative is a circle formation with some students sitting on chairs or on the carpet and others on desks behind them, with as few students as possible having their backs to other members of the class.

Whole Class Discussion

Whole Class discussion helps develop group cohesion and exposes students to a wide range of ideas, views and opinions.

It is useful to distinguish between class discussions which are essentially concerned with sharing (Whole Class discussions), sessions with the whole class in which the teacher uses questioning as the major technique of learning (Whole Class question and answer sessions) and times when the teacher is delivering information to the class (Whole Class input sessions).

Whole Class discussion is most likely to succeed if the emphasis is on students communicating to each other and to their teacher the ideas, opinions and understandings which they have developed about the subject.

Therefore, students need:

- to be able to clarify their thinking or to develop some understanding of the subject matter **before** the Whole Class session - by making notes, drawing pictures or talking in pairs or small groups

- to understand the purpose and anticipated outcomes of the discussion.

Teachers need:

- to make sure that the classroom furniture is arranged so that all students can see each other

- to encourage students to practise basic communication techniques, such as:

  - looking at the people to whom they are talking

  - listening carefully to others and thinking about what they say

  - referring to what other class members have said

  - mentioning those referred to by name when appropriate.

Class discussions are unlikely to contribute to the development of students' talking and listening abilities if:

- only a few students become involved in them

- most students have the opportunity only to speak briefly

- they tend to be dominated by the most vocal students

- the teacher tends to control who speaks and determines the value of each student's contribution

- students speak to the teacher rather than to the rest of the class

- students feel threatened by having to articulate their ideas before they have had the opportunity to test them in a more secure environment.

If teachers use class discussion at an early stage in the learning process, students will need preparation time for exploratory talk or writing. Indeed, spontaneous Whole Class discussions should be the exception rather than the rule.

Ideally, class discussions should be planned for the later stages of the learning process so that students can articulate, to a responsive yet critical audience, ideas and opinions which they have carefully thought through. The best class discussions are likely to be those in which the teacher either contributes as an equal participant or else withdraws from the discussion and asks a class member to chair the session. The latter alternative is more likely to occur at upper primary or secondary levels, with the length of the discussion being determined by the experience and maturity of the students.

Questioning

Questioning needs close attention because it occupies so much classroom time - most oral interactions between teacher and students take the form of question and response. Typically, teachers already know the answers to the questions they ask. Traditional question and answer sessions are, therefore, not occasions for genuine communication as part of a learning act.

Research findings into teacher questioning of whole classes indicate that in very many classrooms:

- seventy per cent of the talking is done by the teacher

- the questions asked tend to be low-level ones which only require recall of factual information

- students respond with one word or one sentence answers

- teachers ask questions at an average rate of one every twelve seconds

- very few teachers allow more than one second before expecting a response

- question asking is largely the province of teachers

- on some occasions when the question posed appears to offer a wider range of response, teachers will accept only one answer.

The emphasis in Whole Class question and answer sessions is on students communicating what they know to their teacher. For teachers concerned with developing their students' ability to communicate, these sessions leave much to be desired. There is little opportunity for students to express their thoughts because of the amount of teacher talk and because only one student can talk at a time. In any case, the situation does not lend itself to students talking in an extended way.

The opportunity for conversation and argument in which teacher and student engage in **developing** ideas is also denied.

Questioning sessions conducted in this way provide very little time for students to think, nor are the kinds of questions posed thought-provoking. Consequently they offer few opportunities for students to use talk in order to learn. At best, they will be frustrating for the student who becomes engaged - but is denied the opportunity to make more of what comes up.

Wait time

Teachers can improve questioning sessions by asking open, rather than closed, questions, and by allowing students adequate time to answer.

Wait time refers to the period of time that is deliberately allowed to elapse between:

- the teacher's question and a student's response, or

- the student's response and any comment from the teacher.

Very few teachers wait more than one second after a question before making a further teaching move, such as rephrasing the question or naming a student to answer it. And yet a wait time of three to five seconds is needed for students to think about what has been discussed and formulate a response.

Wait time, when applied consistently, can be a very simple yet effective means of giving students time to produce more thoughtful answers, comments or opinions. It often results in a more reflective environment for discussion, particularly if it is combined with open questions beyond the literal level.

Thinking time

A worthwhile strategy, which extends the concept of wait time, involves the teacher allowing a pause of between thirty and sixty seconds before expecting students to answer questions.

To use this strategy effectively, teachers will need to:

- explain the strategy and its purpose to their students, stressing that the pause provides thinking time in which to generate a response to the question

- ensure that they ask questions which require careful thought

- provide variety by insisting on silent contemplation on some occasions and by allowing talk in pairs or small groups at other times.

A longer wait or thinking time should draw from students lengthier and more thoughtful responses, more high level thinking and more attentive listening. It should also encourage teachers to listen more carefully to what their students have to say.

Teacher action during each stage of the learning process

Engagement	Exploration
• encourages reflection	• facilitates development of group skills
• reviews progress so far	• provides time for students to make their own links with the information
• points to further directions	• may provide time for individual writing for this purpose
• poses organising questions	• may provide direction through open-ended questioning
• encourages prediction and hypothesising	• monitors small group talk closely - does not contribute
• presents new content material	• reflects on information gained from monitoring student talk
• links new material with old	
• provides structured overview	
• demonstrates or models new skills	

Teacher action during each stage of the learning process

Transformation	Presentation	Reflection
• recalls directions	• provides sense of performance by explicitly valuing the work produced	• reviews products and outcomes of learning
• sets Transformation activities		• reviews the learning process
• organises classroom appropriately	• ensures products have been shaped to suit given audience and purpose	• shows enthusiasm and disappointment
• reviews constraints		• encourages students to evaluate their own progress in terms of curriculum aims
• facilitates development of writing, reading and speaking skills, as appropriate	• organises classroom appropriately	
• directs students to best resource material	• encourages audience response and feedback	• organises classroom appropriately for:

• monitors students' progress and understanding	• encourages sharing of products	- individual writing
		  - small group talk
		  - whole class discussion

• monitors quality of work produced	• facilitates development of presentation skills, such as:	• re-establishes links between this activity and whole curriculum

• provides new information where necessary (by recycling the Engagement and Exploration Stages)	- handwriting
	  - layout and design
	  - editing/proofing
	  - rehearsal
	  - public speaking
	  - oral reading
		• solicits student ideas on follow-up activities, future directions and extension work

• records progress of students	• evaluates products of students in terms of goals (where necessary)	• reflects upon all this for future planning

Note:
- side by side helps sharing and co-operation

- pairs facing pairs facilitates interaction.

5 Getting Started

Successful small group work in the classroom **doesn't just happen**. It depends upon the degree to which teachers understand how to operate small groups, the commitment they have to their success, and the extent to which students regard working in groups as a significant learning strategy. Experience will enhance the teacher's understanding of how to help students learn in small groups, just as it will develop the students' ability to work effectively in them.

This chapter outlines some possible ways for teachers to introduce their students to the concept of group work in order to help improve the quality of learning in the classroom.

The need for order

Undertaking small group work with a class that seems to need discipline may appear to demand too much time and effort from teachers. However, this view reflects a common misconception that small group work is uncontrolled. Nothing could be further from the truth. Organising the classroom into small groups gives teachers more control over both the learning and classroom discipline. Teachers are in a position to hear and see what their students are thinking and doing much more effectively than when they are working with the whole class as a single unit.

Many teachers find that discipline in the classroom improves when students operate in small groups because all are involved in discussion or the work of the classroom. The immediate responsibility they feel to other group members can promote **self** discipline more effectively than any feeling of responsibility towards the teacher.

Sharing the theory

Teachers should tell students what they're going to be doing and why. This will give purpose to the activities that follow. Students should also be reminded frequently to reflect on how their handling and understanding of the **process** is developing.

It is also important and worthwhile to discuss the small group approach with the school administration. This should enable teachers to negotiate a more supportive environment for the early stages.

A gradual beginning

Teachers may well find that their confidence in managing small groups will increase if they begin gradually (and with their best classes in the secondary school). Like students, teachers need to practise when learning new techniques and skills, and they also need to have a supportive atmosphere in which to learn - one in which they are not afraid to make mistakes. For these reasons, teachers who are learning to use small group work in the classroom should begin in the mornings, when both they and their students are fresh and alert.

Students who have little experience with small group work may find it a shock to change suddenly from sitting quietly in rows and paying attention to the teacher to sitting in small groups and being **asked** to talk. An over-reaction to the perceived freedom of small groups must be expected. This can be defused, to a large extent, by careful planning of small group activities and the use of a **gradual** settling-in process.

As a first step from individual work, plan for short, specific and purposeful work in pairs. Reading each other's stories or notes, testing each other on number combinations, or checking each other's methods are simple and well-tried activities that help students learn to listen to and assist each other.

Still using pairs, gradually incorporate into lessons the type of exploratory talk that allows students to make sense of new information. For example, the following will give students practice in valuing their own talk and experience as it relates to what is taught in school: a simple direction to explain to a partner the algorithm that has just been described on the board, an instruction to discuss a technical term which has been mentioned for the first time, an invitation to tell about a time in your own life that relates to a description of a hospital that has just been read. These sessions should be kept very short, only two to three minutes to begin with, and should be incorporated frequently into lessons as they develop. In this way, the value of talking to help learning is stressed through overt teacher action and instruction.

Remember that to somebody not in a small group (like the teacher), the early stages of exploratory talk can often sound as though the group is wandering away from the task. However, teachers should be wary of stopping a group if it appears to be digressing, or if the discussion seems irrelevant to the topic, or even repetitious and slow. Exploration is a time when students can relate new information to their own experience, and often that experience **will** include memories, anecdotes or references to television shows. Keeping exploratory sessions short at the beginning will save headaches for the teacher.

Transformation and Presentation tasks can be started as activities for pairs too - with the concept of a larger group being developed along the way. For example, dividing up the activities to be done in mathematics, and having partners check each other's work before swapping with another pair for marking, will save time in the lesson, as well as allowing the teacher to identify the problems that arise in discussion. This organisation also ensures that students' initial experience in a small group is both purposeful and well-structured.

As the teacher's confidence and understanding grows, so will his or her ability to use and structure this sort of interaction. And as the students' involvement in the lesson grows, the teacher's confidence is boosted still further.

Organising the Classroom

When learning to use small groups, teachers may find the following points about organisation helpful.

Size of groups

Except at the Presentation Stage, when combinations of six, or on rare occasions eight, are useful, groups should consist of four members - with a pair sitting alongside each other, directly opposite another pair.

Once the room has been organised so that all students can see the board (see p. 40), the teacher needs to allow some settling-down time. Friendship groups may sometimes be larger than four, and a decision will have to be made about whether five students should work as one group or as a three and a pair. Teachers faced with a friendship group of six or more should request that those students form two smaller groups.

Keep tasks short

Keep all group tasks **short** when starting. Suitable activities might include:

- making a group list
- finding the main points in a paragraph
- predicting the results of an experiment or the end of a story
- checking that every person in the group knows what to do next, and so on.

All of these short and directed group tasks can be given by the teacher who is learning the ropes of small group management.

Don't expect instant success

Teachers should be aware that instant success is rare. There will be students who don't **like** to work in groups, some whose school experience has led them to perceive any situation where the teacher is not making them work as an excuse not to work, and others who are just plain naughty. Yet teachers should be wary of blaming the students for their lack of expertise in handling the small group situation. This is tantamount to saying,'They're not succeeding with group work at present, so I won't give them any chance to get better'.

Managing those who won't work in groups

Teachers should explain to their class that students who won't work in groups - for whatever reason - don't work in groups. Desks for students who are disruptive, or for students who choose to work alone, should be provided in the classroom (see diagram on p. 40). Opportunities for these isolated students to share their thoughts and work with other students can be organised on a short-term basis.

It is important for teachers to know how to help students learn to work in the small group situation. Very young children will often be exaggeratedly polite to each other in the early stages of group work - and many junior primary teachers know the value of group play to help overcome a reluctance to share.

Older students are often inconsiderate and self-centred, unwilling to accept challenges to their ideas or corrections to their work. And so it is valuable for groups to reflect upon their own group process when the teacher perceives a need for it. Questions for this type of reflection might be as simple as, *What does your group do when you've finished the task early?* or as potentially illuminating as, *How does your group deal with interruptions when you're working?*

This type of reflection can be a quick, spontaneous event or it can become a group research topic, with the group reporting their findings over a week. But it still places the responsibility for both the behaviour and the work in the classroom on the students and on the group, rather than on the teacher.

Handling disruptions

Teachers beginning group work with their classes will find that they are moving around the room constantly - monitoring groups, giving directions and clarifying misconceptions for particular groups. When the need arises to steer a group back to work, it is important that the teacher moves directly to the group concerned and does not call out across other working groups. There is nothing to be gained from stopping the work of nine groups to chastise one group or even one or two students.

When eight(or nine!) groups are misbehaving, the best thing to save both the teacher's peace of mind and the students' time is to stop them all.

The problem may lie:

- with the task
  - it may be unclear
  - too hard
  - boring
  - perceived as irrelevant
  - too slight for the time given

- outside the classroom
  - a lunch-time fight
  - a perception of unfairness
  - a lack of commitment or energy
  - individual personal problems.

However, it is generally impossible for the teacher to gauge the reasons on the spot. It is sometimes useful to ask students to stop work and consider the reasons for their lack of attention and effort - and discuss these before returning to the task. As a last resort, it may be necessary to intervene with direct whole class instruction. This does not, however, represent **better** teaching and learning; it is merely a fall-back disciplinary intervention - a pause in the healthy learning process.

Teachers can also refer individual problems to other support staff within the school or region.

The value of a tape recorder

A tape recorder is a very useful aid. Students who are unused to having their talk valued by the teacher need to have that sense of value reinforced. When teachers record a small group's talk and use what was said during the discussion as the basis for comment the next day, students can see that what **they** bring to the lesson is just as important as what they are given.

Teachers, of course, can learn many things about their own classroom performance by listening to a series of such tapes. This is an excellent and relatively simple method of getting to know exactly what goes on after students have been asked to work together.

Students, too, will often be impressed by how much ground they have covered without being conscious of it.

Reporting back sessions

Teachers should be wary of extended reporting back sessions at the end of group work. When all students have been discussing the same topic, or doing the same experiment, sums or exercises, both they and their teacher should be spared the boredom of repetition. The reports, summaries or answers of one or two groups will provide enough information for other groups to check their work or compare their results. The teacher, having moved around the classroom **during** the group work, does not need to use the reporting back time to check that the work has been done.

The time wasted by having all groups report back to the class is better spent discussing any differences or conflict that may have arisen between groups' results.

When groups have been working on different material, there is often a real need and reason for reporting to other class members. The diagrams on pp. 29 and 35 suggest methods for reporting back, or presenting work to the whole class, that should be more effective than repetitive Whole Class report sessions.

Sample Lessons for Introducing Small Group Work

The following lessons are designed to enhance students' understanding of how groups work. At the same time, they stress students' responsibility for controlling their own learning. Awareness of how one goes about learning is essential for learners to realise their own potential to learn - outside school as well as in the classroom.

The lesson plans give step-by-step procedures which teachers should find useful for helping students to come to value their own roles in their learning. They may be taken up as outlined, or adapted to suit the age level of a particular class.

Lesson 1: students as learners

(a) Tell the class that you will be spending forty minutes finding out how they learn best. Define learning as coming to new understandings or acquiring new knowledge for oneself.

(b) Ask the students to write down, individually, the six ways they consider are best for them to learn.

(5 minutes)

(c) Ask them, in Home Groups of four, to take turns reading out their lists.

(5 minutes)

(d) While they are doing this, give each Home Group a large piece of paper and ask them to make a group list of all their ideas.

(5 minutes)

(e) Tell the class that they have ten minutes to organise their group lists so that the most important idea has four stars, and so on. Walk around the class and listen to what the groups are saying.

(10 minutes)

(f) Pin up the lists so that all the class can see them. Where necessary, ask students to clarify items for the whole class. Compare lists and allow groups to pose questions to other groups.

(5 minutes)

(g) Ask students to write down individually, for the teacher, a statement of how they think they learn best.

(5 minutes)

(h) Ask students to compare their statements with the individual lists of six points they made earlier, and then ask them to reflect on whether working in small groups has helped them in this activity.

(5 minutes)

Lesson 2: working in small groups

(a) Tell the class that you will allow forty minutes for them to formulate their own rules for group discussion.

(b) Ask them to write down, individually, a list of five 'Rules for the Group'.

(5 minutes)

(c) Ask them to share their lists, having given out a large sheet of paper to each Home Group.

(5 minutes)

(d) Ask each Home Group to list on the paper provided those points all members had in common. Then they are to discuss the other points, either adding them to the group list or omitting them according to the group's decision.

(10 minutes)

(e) Form Sharing Groups by combining two groups. Each Home Group should explain its list. Groups can add to or delete from their own lists.

(10 minutes)

(f) Pin up all Home Group lists at the front of the room, and on a new sheet of paper make a heading, 'Rules for Group Work'. All points that are common to every group can be listed as class rules. Each group is then asked to remember their own rules and the class rules in future group discussions.

(10 minutes)

Lesson 3: effective and ineffective groups

This third activity can be undertaken when students have had some practice at working in small groups. It should promote reflection on the group process, and further develop understanding of the learning process.

(a) Tell students that you are going to spend forty minutes to increase the effectiveness of their small group work.

(b) Before they talk, ask the students to write for a few minutes about what they consider to be important for a group to function well.

(5 minutes)

(c) Ask them to discuss in their Home Groups what they consider to be the characteristics of:

- an effective group
- an ineffective group.

(10 minutes)

(d) Each student takes notes during the discussion, and at the end of ten minutes, two members of each Home Group change with two members of another group. In the Sharing Groups students compare lists and make a new, composite list.

(10 minutes)

(e) Hand out the list of 'Characteristics of Effective and Ineffective Groups' (p. 69), or an adaptation, and ask the Sharing Groups to compare it with their own lists.

(10 minutes)

(f) Share your own reflections on the way the groups in the class are working, referring to the criteria on the handout sheet.

(5 minutes)

Sample Introductory Lessons for Junior Primary Classes

The teacher should choose an appropriate context for these introductory activities, and prepare the day's work to include a variety of small group tasks.

Lesson 1: students as learners

(a) After morning news or welcome, call the class to the mat to tell them that they are going to start learning how to work together in small groups. Explain why you have decided to do this and praise their good work that has led you to make this decision.

(5 minutes)

(b) Ask the students to tell their neighbours why they think it might be a good idea to work together in this way.

(2 minutes)

(c) Students share ideas with Whole Class. Make a list of the suggestions and pin it up so that all students can see it.

(5 minutes)

(d) In a Whole Class discussion ask the students to think about the work they did the previous day on a particular topic and to answer the following questions:

- Did they ask each other for help?
- Did they help their friends?
- What sort of things did they need to ask the teacher?
- Could they have asked each other instead?
- Who did they show their work to when they had finished?

(10 minutes)

Lesson 2: working in small groups

(a) Tell the students that they are going to work in Home Groups, and (depending on the class) either allocate them to groups that will work well together, or allow them to form friendship groups of four.

(5 minutes)

(b) Ask the Home Groups to arrange their desks and chairs so that each student can see the blackboard without having to turn around. Check the furniture arrangements and ensure that any changes are understood by the groups.

(5 minutes)

(c) Ask the students in their Home Groups to write or talk about why they are moving into groups and how they feel about working this way. If they are writing, they might commence 'Today we moved the furniture...'

(10 minutes)

(d) Ask the students to read their accounts to the others in their group. Walk around the class and listen to what the groups are saying.

(5 minutes)

Lesson 3: working in small groups

(a) Ask each Home Group to decide on four rules for group work. If time permits, students should consider which of their rules is most important.

(10 minutes)

(b) List each group's rules on the blackboard as part of a class list. Draw attention to any rules which the groups have in common. In a Whole Class discussion, talk about which rules the students think are most important. Make alterations and additions as necessary to the class list.

(5 minutes)

(c) Under the heading 'Rules for Group Work', write down the amended list and pin it up so that all students can see it.

Characteristics of Effective and Ineffective Groups

Effective Groups

1. The atmosphere tends to be informal, comfortable. People are involved and interested.

2. There is a lot of discussion in which everyone takes part. Everyone keeps to the point.

3. Everybody understands the task they have to do.

4. The group members listen to each other. Every idea is given a hearing.

5. There is disagreement. The group is comfortable with this, and works towards sorting it out. Nobody feels unhappy with decisions made.

6. People feel free to criticise and say honestly what they think.

7. Everybody knows how everybody else feels about what is being discussed.

8. When action needs to be taken, everyone is clear about what has to be done, and they help each other.

9. Different people take over the role of leader from time to time.

10. The group is conscious of how well it is working and of what is interfering with its progress. It can look after itself.

Ineffective Groups

1. The atmosphere reflects indifference or boredom.

2. Only one or two people talk. Little effort is made to keep to the point of the discussion.

3. It is difficult to understand what the group task is.

4. People do not really listen to each other. Some ideas are not put forward to the group.

5. Disagreements are not dealt with effectively. They are put to the vote without being discussed. Some people are unhappy with decisions.

6. People are not open about what they are thinking. They grumble about decisions afterwards.

7. One or two people are dominant. What they say goes.

8. Nobody takes any interest in what has to be done, and nobody offers to help others.

9. Only one or two people make the decisions and act as group leaders.

10. The group does not talk about how it is working or about the problems it is facing. It needs someone to look after it.

Adapted from Douglas McGregor, *Characteristics of Effective and Ineffective Groups.*

Note:

- teacher monitors Sharing Group talk and outcomes without disturbing group interaction
- three groups can be monitored from this position
- it's easy to see which students are working

- students working alone.

6 Problems

This chapter deals with some of the problems that teachers often perceive when they are beginning to implement small group work in their classes. The problems are expressed here as questions that are commonly asked about small group work, followed by an explanation or response.

How do you know all students are working?

Usually the teacher can tell whether or not a group is working by looking at the students' faces and posture. If they're absorbed, they are likely to be working. Monitoring what they are saying is another way of finding out, and sometimes just listening to their tone is enough. The teacher has a much better chance of finding out exactly what students are thinking if they are allowed to say what they think, and so, in effect, small group work makes it easier for the teacher to know just what students are doing and thinking. However, the teacher cannot be with all groups at once and, to some extent, students have to be trusted.

When should you interrupt a small group's working?

One of the most difficult problems that teachers face is knowing when and how much to interfere with the work going on in small groups. Generally, teachers should interrupt only when they believe it is essential because whenever any outsider comes into a group its work is disrupted.

It is best for teachers not to become too deeply involved with the work of any one group, as they need to be aware of what is happening in all groups in the classroom. When asked to explain something, it is generally best to respond as quickly and clearly as possible. Giving students the information they want is preferable to attempting to draw the information from them by questioning.

What about the disruptive student?

There will always be some students who either seek to disrupt, or cannot help disrupting, the work of the classroom. Small group work will not bring about an immediate change in this type of behaviour. None the less it may help to reduce teachers' problems as these students become more actively involved in learning and feel the influence of their peers.

There are no perfect answers to the problem of disruption because of its complex causes. However, the teacher can provide an isolation desk for disruptive students, and can tell the student that she or he is being isolated for a particular period because of disruptive behaviour.

One disadvantage of this solution is that the more often a student is isolated, the less opportunity he or she has to experience co-operative behaviour within a group. So it is recommended primarily when it's important that the disruptive student does not disturb the work of others.

At the end of any period of isolation, the teacher should discuss the matter and give the student the opportunity to talk about how she or he feels.

If there is a group of disruptive students in a particular class, try having them work together. The teacher can build on peer identification by telling them that if they want to work together, they will have to work well. Peer pressure can be a valuable aid for the teacher using small groups, and disruptive students are generally those who least want to be the only ones with nothing to present to the rest of the class.

If most of the class is working well in small groups, allowing the disruptive students to work together also permits the teacher to give more time to individuals needing attention.

Some students are disruptive because of their inability to handle the work set for them. They learn early that the best way to avoid failure is not to try. But the small group situation allows students the chance to seek help from their friends, and to make use of ideas generated by the group. If the teacher selects tasks that are clearly within the group's capability, the successful operation of the group, as well as the attitude of the students, will be enhanced.

Do all students have to work in small groups?

Small group work is not offered as a universal panacea for all education's ills. Of course there are students who won't work - even in small groups. Getting these students involved in learning is an extremely complex problem, which won't be solved simply by changing the learning style of the classroom.

Some students choose to work on their own because they feel they can work better like that. If students choose to work in a particular way, and are given the freedom to do so, then they will be committed to making a success of it. The important thing is for teachers to provide the best learning situation for each student. A student can be a solitary worker within a group quite often, and very easily, as she or he feels the need.

What about noise?

The excitement of small group talk does, at times, result in noise. Many teachers avoid using small groups because they are concerned about comments from their colleagues about noise levels. It is hardly surprising that students at a school where this attitude prevails will consider group work as a chance to gossip rather than as an opportunity to learn.

However, where small group work is an important and regular part of the learning process in the classroom, students quickly learn to work without excessive noise.

There should be only one person talking in each group at any particular time, and as long as the students are seated close to each other, there is no reason for them to speak loudly. As students become more familiar with operating in small groups, they work more quietly. Teacher expectation will also influence how quietly students work. If the teacher is not prepared to accept unproductive or unnecessary noise, students will learn to work quietly.

Although the classroom may be noisier during the Presentation Stage, when groups are combining to share and discuss their findings, the teacher will still decide what noise level is acceptable and what is not. Students are quick to recognise situations when noise will not be tolerated - for instance, when the class next door has a test, or when their teacher is not feeling well.

The better the teacher understands how to operate small groups, the quieter and more business-like the classroom will be. The better the students understand that their learning in small groups is purposeful and useful, the more quietly they will work.

What about lower ability students in heterogeneous classes?

In most situations, individuals seldom contribute equally. One need only observe effective groups in operation to see how different students adopt different roles, how they switch roles on occasions, and how the quality of listening is enhanced by working in small groups. Each group member's contribution takes a different form. The person who takes the role of devil's advocate, who asks the question or makes the comment that pushes the group's understanding further has as much to contribute as the person who talks the most.

The presence of a less able student often means that the others need to explain and clarify what she or he does not understand. So, at the same time, this student is helping **them** to understand more clearly what they are talking about.

Less able students are more likely to become engaged in the learning process if they have opportunities to become involved in helping the group achieve its goals than if they are required to listen passively to the teacher, copy notes from the board, or fill in meaningless exercises or worksheets.

Although not all members of a group may appear to be contributing equally, both talented and less able students will benefit from working together. In junior primary classes this is especially so. Younger or less able students receive enormous benefit from those who are just a little more competent than they are. The reciprocal advantage to the ones who have newly mastered a skill or understanding, in demonstrating or explaining it to their peers, is similarly great.

What about students who dominate small groups?

Students who dominate small groups are generally those who dominate a Whole Class discussion. One possible solution to the problem of dominant students is to put them together in one group. Another strategy is for the teacher to structure activities so as to keep the dominant student quiet - for example, the student may be asked to be chairperson in a panel discussion or timekeeper for an experiment.

Students' reflection on how well their group has functioned should also increase their understanding of how to work successfully in small groups. This kind of reflection also helps dominating students to understand the effect they have on a group's operation. Sometimes this is the means by which they discover that they **are** dominating.

However, there are no easy answers to the problem of the dominant student. The best solution is to develop, in students, an understanding of how to work together successfully and purposefully. For older students, written reflection on the working of the group can be helpful. So can discussing the matter orally with junior primary classes.

Note:
- Sharing Group of six
- each student has own copy of notes

- students working individually in Home Group.

Note:

- two groups combine for Presentation; audience does not have to be Whole Class
- Presentation does not have to involve teacher - student to student works well
- desks arranged so that students are as close together as possible: eight chairs, four desks to ensure ease of interaction

- students present to Whole Class so teacher is not sole judge
- eye contact between audience and presenters.

7 Programming and Planning

Programming and planning for the learning that is to take place during the school year is one of the most important tasks which teachers undertake. Programmes of work serve both as the texts from which teachers work, and as a record that reflects their professional growth. They also document the thinking that teachers do and the decisions that they make about learning in their classrooms.

Planning for small group work does not require a major alteration to individual programming styles. Rather, it involves an attempt to articulate the knowledge and understanding that teachers have of how children learn, using the learning framework (outlined in Chapter Two) to help structure and sequence learning activities in the classroom. The following notes and suggestions for programming may prove helpful for teachers when implementing this approach to small group work.

The context determines the classroom structure

Planning small group work involves thinking about three important questions.

- Why should I use small groups?

- When should I use small groups? (And when should I not use them?)

- How should I use small group work?

Programming is very much a decision-making process, through which the teacher determines how best to help students learn in a classroom context. The classic set of questions to be considered in determining a programme is this.

Why ?	(Why are we doing what we're doing?)
What ?	(What are we doing?)
How ?	(How are we going to do it?)
When ?	(When and in what order are we going to do it?)
Who ?	(Who is doing what?)

For whom ?   (Who is our audience?)
Where from ?   (How does this work connect with what we've done before?)
Where to ?   (Where do we go from here?)
How well ?   (What is the quality of our learning?)

Yet it is the relationship **between** these factors that determines the effectiveness of the programme in action. It is not just a matter of deciding to use small groups for this or that activity. The decision to employ small group work is an answer to the 'How will I teach?' question. But the effectiveness and appropriateness of small groups depend on a complex interplay of 'how' with other factors.

The answers to the set of nine questions determine the **context** for small group work. And of all the keys to the problem of 'why, when and how', the learning model is the main one. At each stage of the movement from Engagement to Reflection, students are involved in very different processes - which, in turn, require varying classroom structures and settings.

Exploring a new idea is not the same process as presenting a known idea; receiving information is not the same as transforming it and applying it to a new problem; and so on. Different pieces of content **may** require different learning strategies, but different stages of the learning model certainly do. In other words, the **how** of learning will determine what is learned (as distinct from what is taught) as much as the content being studied.

A concrete illustration makes the point.

- A Year 4 class is programmed to study a science unit on the planet Earth in the solar system. The teacher begins the unit by talking briefly about the Earth being in space, with the sun visible by day and the moon and stars by night. She poses some questions which the class will be answering through the unit of study.

  For this Engagement session the class is a single group, facing the teacher at the blackboard. Why a whole class **now**, for **this** activity? Because the teacher needs to give the same information to all the students, at the same time, and they don't need to be interacting. Individually but collectively, they are receiving.

- The teacher now asks the class to work in their Home Groups of four, to talk and make their own notes about what they already know of the Earth in the solar system, and the relationship between the Earth, moon and sun. Why Home Groups **now**, for **this** activity? Because the students need to generate ideas and reflect on their current state of knowledge. Interaction is called for because it generates a wider range of ideas; all the students can participate actively; they are not teacher-dependent; along the way they will become curious and uncertain and perhaps even disagree with each other - all of which engages their intention to learn. They will also deal with some of the questions which arise from their investigations, particularly when they are at unequal stages in their knowledge of the subject (children are great teachers of other children!); and the topic, which begins as the teacher's, becomes theirs too.

The Whole Class group can't possibly achieve all this equally well, and in the same time frame, and nor can each student working alone, in silence, at a desk.

And so it goes on. The point is that different processes and settings produce different learning outcomes, even with the same material.

Questions to be considered when planning

The best approach to planning is to work backwards; first to consider the desired outcomes (always in students' learning terms) and then to ask oneself which processes and settings will best help the students achieve those outcomes. The significant difference is between the approach which says 'What do I want to teach my class?' and that which says 'What learning outcomes do I want my students to achieve?' The crucial **how to get there** question is likely to be answered very differently in each case.

The teacher unused to small group work in the classroom will inevitably have to confront certain questions. The combination of the learning model and the small group processes recommended in this book should enable the teacher to deal constructively with such questions as:

- When should I plan to intervene in small group work and address the whole class?

- When do the students shift from Whole Class to Home Groups to Sharing Groups and so on?

- Which activities work best in small groups, when and why?

- If the class is in small groups, how do I get all the students to the same end-point, and at the same time?

- How can all the students make a presentation to others, without it taking forever or becoming hugely boring and repetitive for the listeners?

- When is it more efficient and effective in learning terms to talk to the whole class?

- How can I generate more time and opportunity to work with students on a one-to-one basis, without losing the rest of the class or holding them up?

If teachers understand what small groups can do, they should be able to answer these questions and then make decisions on the appropriate classroom structure at each stage of the learning model.

Goals

Programming for learning in small groups involves establishing both process goals and content goals.

Process goals

Process goals refer to the type of social and emotional milieu that the teacher wants to build up, over time, within the classroom, so that everybody who works together in the room knows how to behave and interact harmoniously. Important goals such as courtesy, self-esteem, respect for others, encouragement of curiosity, acceptance of individual differences and enjoyment in learning - all those intangibles which make up classroom atmosphere or tone - are involved here. These are things which cannot be taken for granted, but need to be worked at, and towards, constantly.

Teachers need to take account of the processes of learning that operate in their classrooms and to programme specific activities that will help students to learn these processes. Then students will be able to learn without hindrance the content material which teachers want to teach. In a classroom operating on the principles of small group learning, the teacher should begin the year with a programme designed to develop students' understandings about small group work, using ideas such as those described in Chapter Five.

Here is a sample programme for the first week of the school year, in which the teacher is aiming to establish the learning environment so that students begin to learn and understand the processes of small group work and other classroom structures by practising them.

Term 1 programme: 'Getting to know you'

Appropriate, with adaptations, for Years 3-7.

Aims Over the first three weeks of school, the students will learn how to work effectively in small groups. They will develop group process skills through a gradual build-up of collaborative learning activities based on the theme of 'Getting to know you', while the teacher gets to know them.

Specific aims include setting up classroom routines for reading, writing, talk, homework, behaviour, mathematics, science, social studies, health and art within an integrated curriculum.

WEEK 1

LANGUAGE

Context Pairs interviewing and reporting - family, things enjoyed most at school last year, things to work on this year, favourite books, hobbies, and so on. Children seated in friendship groups/pairs.

Engagement 1 Teacher talks a little about herself, invites children in pairs to make up two questions they would like to ask her.

Exploration Teacher asks pairs to discuss what she has said, and to rehearse questions for each of them to ask someone else.

Transformation Pairs combine to form groups of four. Each person interviews one of the other pair, and introduces new partner to the small group.

Engagement 2 Teacher negotiates and demonstrates the writing of a factual introductory statement about herself on an overhead transparency, using ideas generated from her oral introduction and student questions.

Presentation Individuals write about their partners for presentation on display board. Final copy to be ready for Thursday.

Reflection Students discuss the following questions in small groups. What did you learn about listening to others? How will that be helpful in your work this year? Students generate their own rules for group work.

MATHS (Measurement)

Engagement Examine wall space for class introductions mural: dimensions, units of measurement, counting, class numbers.

Exploration Estimate and measure dimensions of paper needed to make life-size cut-out of partner; estimate and measure length needed for cut-outs of Home Group.

Engagement Number concepts - half, quarter, height, units of measurement, counting - revision and practice.

Transformation Groups divide paper, and members outline each other.

ART

Transformation Self-portrait on life-size cut-out.

Presentation Small groups arrange display of own figures, design background for mural.

Reflection Students discuss the following questions. Were there any problems in our groups? How can these be overcome? Review rules for group work - do these work all the time?

SOCIAL STUDIES

Engagement Students share rules for group work. Teacher discussses notion of rules for groups of people. Common social rules, such as the Ten Commandments, school rules, bicycle safety and library rules can be used here, as appropriate for year level.

Exploration Groups decide which rules they agree/disagree with, giving reasons.

Transformation Groups draft contributions to a set of class rules they can abide by this year (4+ rules per group).

Presentation Small groups combine, share rules and decide on six to be included in class wall chart/big book/individual cards.

LANGUAGE

Engagement Teacher-led discussion of conventions of format decided upon for presentation of class rules, and of appropriate language styles.

Exploration Students draft and share formulations of class rules, and their own group rules.

Transformation Revision and final drafting with printing (or handwriting) practice.

Presentation Pairs swap for checking and proofreading. Final presentations of class rules in chart or big book. Reading and discussion of the rules, and their implications.

Reflection Small groups discuss the following questions. What have you learnt about working in groups so far - in this classroom? In other situations? Whole class sharing of ideas.

Engagement Individuals read introductions written by partners, correct and approve for publication.

Transformation Final drafts of partner-introductions; preparation of personal written introduction using same format.

Presentation Whole Class session of students reading their introductions; completion of mural by pasting partner and self-introductions to cut-out shapes.

The following sequence is designed to encourage reflection on the learning process.

Engagement Teacher introduces reflection journals.

Exploration Small groups discuss reflection journals, familiarising themselves with the idea and clarifying it.

Transformation Pairs discuss the introductions experience, then individuals reflect in journals on this and the first week of school.

Presentation Whole Class discussion of reflections on the first week.

Content goals

The long-term content goals of any programme are generally determined by the teacher, either through discussion of a school or subject policy, or by reference to a prescribed or recommended syllabus. These goals are for the most part prescriptive, and can be seen as a statement of overall intention on the part of the teacher, the subject department or the school. The programme, then, is an expression of the teacher's attempt to help students achieve these learning outcomes.

Short-term process goals and the content aims of individual units of work should be clearly stated within the framework of long-term goals, but they need not be rigid. As long as the teacher has a clear idea of the desired outcomes by the end of a unit, term and year, then the freedom to alter, adapt or even scrap a particular programme can be enjoyed and utilised.

The process of learning determines student outcomes, as much as content or aims - and as students develop their understandings of small group work over time, process considerations have a tendency to modify short-term aims and objectives.

Teachers may find, for example, that small group activities they have planned take longer than expected, take different directions from those anticipated, or lead children away from the intended goal. In these cases, it is up to the teacher who is monitoring and evaluating the work in the classroom to decide whether to intervene and guide students back to the planned path or to follow the direction of the students.

Evaluating the work accomplished and revising programmes to record changes that have occurred will ensure that the short-term goals of any particular programme are not overlooked and that long-term goals are reached.

Catering for the needs of individual students

Where teachers know in advance that some class members have specific problems, interests or abilities, they can take these into account when programming for small groups. The small group situation makes it easier for teachers to help less able students, provides room for students to follow their particular interests, and allows easily for extension of more capable students. Of course, it is essential that teachers prepare lessons carefully to ensure that students are given tasks suitable to their abilities, needs and interests. And it is only during the time that teachers give to lesson preparation that the interrelationship of individual activities can be evaluated and built on for future planning.

If students' learning is to develop over a school year, the progress of the programme must be carefully monitored. This means that teachers need to review and reflect on the ways in which the planned and unplanned work of the classroom has led to the desired short-term and long-term learning outcomes.

This is particularly the case when individual students are facing difficulties. The teacher may need to provide one-to-one attention, assistance and support, which must be programmed in advance to make sure that the teacher has the time to work in this way.

Planning for small group interaction

When teachers wish to programme for small group interaction, the form of Presentation will often dictate the way in which groups are arranged, and this should be considered when programming. A whole-class presentation, for example, will mean that all members of the class need to be free to work, listen, and respond at the same time. The teacher needs to have planned carefully so that this will happen.

A presentation by one group to another, whether the work is in progress or in completed form, need not interrupt the rest of the class if the teacher has planned for it and the timing and classroom movement are expected. Similarly, when students are presenting their work to audiences from outside the classroom, the teacher must plan for the considerable amount of organisation and preparation that is often required beforehand.

At the Transformation Stage, students may want particular resources and equipment and the teacher must plan for their likely needs. This type of planning increases the efficiency of the classroom. At this stage too, as students work towards making new information part of their own knowledge, they will often need help and so the teacher must also plan to be available to give it.

A note on time

When considering how much time small group work seems to take by comparison with direct teacher instruction, it is worth reflecting on the **quality** of learning and the difference between what is taught and what is learned.

Forty minutes of activity which provokes significant student learning is very much more efficient than thirty minutes of teaching which leads to very little effective learning.

Another point to consider is the total amount of time devoted to any one stage of the learning model. It is often the case that extra time allocated to the Exploration and Transformation Stages will lead to a saving of time later on. At the very least, if students become engaged in their learning, repetition and revision will become less necessary.

Allowing for flexibility

The programme is not just a blueprint for action. It is a representation of the teacher's ideas and theory. Planning for student learning should ensure that the teacher knows where the course is heading and how the work is to be covered. And having engaged in thoughtful planning, the teacher should feel confident enough to change or adapt the programme as circumstances require.

A programme may sometimes seem to be unsuccessful because of faults in its construction: students may not have been given enough direction; the resources may prove inadequate; the time allowed may turn out to be too much or too little. On the other hand, students may develop a spontaneous interest in something unexpected. In all such cases, the teacher should feel free to intervene and diverge from the planned programme to cater for any unforeseen difficulties or to build on any unexpected interest.

When divergences occur, 'post-programming' (altering the programme after the event) is useful for reflecting on and evaluating the quality of classroom learning and for providing further direction for future planning.

Note:
- Whole Class discussion without the teacher requires careful planning
- it's what has happened beforehand that makes this work, and breeds this level of engagement

- the group of four is the ideal vehicle for reflection on the learning process.

8 Evaluation and Assessment

Teachers interested in the assessment of small group work should read this chapter in conjunction with the previous one on programming. For valid assessment to take place it is essential to know **what** is being assessed and **why**. Thus, the aims of the programme will, to a large extent, dictate the assessment needed.

The difference between assessment and evaluation

The distinction between assessment and evaluation is an important one. Assessment is a judgement of the quality of student outcomes measured against the learning objectives. Evaluation is a deliberate appraisal of the effectiveness and quality of the teaching and learning that have taken place. It is a process used continually in planning, monitoring, reflecting and post-programming.

Evaluating the work of the classroom

Learning about learning requires planned evaluation by both teacher and students. The Reflection Stage should play an important role in helping students develop as learners and in helping teachers improve their structuring of the learning process.

Teachers are often unaware of how much evaluation is going on as they continually note the progress or problems of particular students and the success or otherwise of their own actions, resource materials, lessons or units of work. According to the results of these on-the-spot evaluations, they are continually changing, adapting, rephrasing or reteaching as the needs of the class demand.

Small group work involves students in evaluation to a much greater extent than when the teacher is directing the class from the front of the room. Groups need to be aware of their own actions. They must be conscious of how they operate and responsible for any changes that they make to their own performance.

The Reflection Stage provides a means for teachers to plan for this type of evaluation. Teachers should also encourage reflection when a group is seen to be in difficulties or is not displaying the common social courtesies that form the most basic rules for all small group interaction.

Students should take some responsibility for the evaluation of their learning in small groups. It is important for the teacher to encourage them in the type of decision-making needed to advance their work. Groups must be aware that some members may work more slowly than others, and allocate specific tasks accordingly. They also need to know that all their work is to be completed for presentation at a certain time, and must organise their activities to that end. Of course, teachers can help in this continuous evaluation of progress by issuing reminders to individuals or to groups.

Checklists, devised by the teacher or by the groups themselves, are often helpful in planning what needs to be done and in reinforcing the ground rules of effective group work.

Checklist 1 Prepared by Students, Year 6 Science
Class topic: Flowering Plants - radio play

A GROWING CYCLE (Andrew, Mario, Mike, Tony)		
1. Script (all)	✓	
2. Editing (all)	✓	finish at home ✓
3. Final Draft	✓	
4. Tape recorder - Tony (Lib.)	✓	Mike !!
5. Tape - Mario (Mr G.)		
6. Practice (all)		
7. Sound FX (music - Andrew * bring mouth organ Mike!)		
8. Recording (all) * Wednesday Period 6 in library		
9. Presentation - Andrew introduces us		
10. Script to Mr G. FRIDAY 24th.		

The student-devised checklist (Example 1) may be useful for regular evaluation when the class is working in this way. The teacher should make explicit why a task is to be approached in a particular way so that students will be better equipped to learn rather than to be taught.

Teacher-devised checklists (Example 2) for evaluating group processes may not be required as often. They are most valuable when they are used to satisfy a need - either when the teacher perceives that a group is not working effectively or when the group asks for help. This type of checklist will not instantly solve problems, but it is a useful reference that focusses students' attention on ways of fixing problems within the group.

Evaluating both progress and process is an essential part of getting things done in the classroom and of creating in students a sense of responsibility for their own learning. It also helps the teacher to monitor very quickly the work of groups and to keep a check on what is happening - and how the programme is developing.

Checklist 2 Prepared for all groups by the teacher

Group Checklist			
	Yes	No	Comments
1. Did everybody participate?			
2. Did anybody feel left out?			
3. Were all members contributing?			
4. Was there any cutting off, or dominating by one person?			
5. Was there any argument? How was it resolved?			
6. Did everybody know what they had to do?			
7. Are you satisfied with the work you have done (so far)?			

Assessing the work of the classroom

The framework for learning can help teachers to assess students' achievements because it provides opportunities to monitor their work at different stages.

Students' exploratory talk or writing should never be marked, though students may often evaluate it for themselves. Exploratory talk and writing are not intended for outside observers: their purpose is to help students learn, and on no account should students be assessed as they work their way towards understanding. The teacher should, however, monitor exploratory talk and gauge from student activity the extent to which individuals are secure and confident in their groups.

There is no reason that work produced for the Presentation Stage **must** be assessed. Equally, assessment need not occur only at the Presentation Stage. Decisions about when and what to assess should be influenced by the teacher's aims and the reasons for the assessment.

The framework for learning is designed to encourage students to suit their presentation to the audience and the purpose required. If that audience is not invariably the teacher-as-examiner, and if the purpose is something other than providing the teacher with a basis for marks, there is a motive for students to draft, edit and refine their work to suit the purpose and the audience selected. And one object of working in small groups is to provide ready access to other people who can help improve the product.

In planning their programmes teachers should decide both what they assess and why they assess it. A Year 6 class, for example, that has prepared stories, based on a unit of the social studies syllabus, for Year 3 children will have little faith in their teacher if they are required to submit them for teacher assessment, instead of presenting them to the audience they were intended for. The next time the teacher suggests they write to the librarian, or compose a letter requesting information, the students will have learned that whatever their stated audience, they are really only writing for the teacher. This does not encourage students to take pains to improve their work. They don't feel a need to make it as good as possible, because they think the teacher will do that for them.

Where the presentation of students' work is designed to give them experience of wider audiences, teacher assessment is invalid unless the students have had feedback and evaluation from the intended audience. This does not pose a great problem. Often a simple discussion with the class about how and when they would like the teacher to assess their work will result in suggestions such as the following:

* The teacher can collect all work after the presentation to the audience for whom it was intended.

* The audience can sometimes be the teacher.

- Group members can select from all the work done over a unit one piece (or three or four) that they would like to submit for teacher assessment.

- The teacher can assess the last draft of the work in progress rather than the final version.

- Other audiences - such as teachers, peers, other classes, parents, visiting experts - can assess the students' work in terms of its aims.

These suggestions, and others that come from discussion, will mean that a variety of methods and styles of assessment and reporting can be incorporated into the teacher's final review of a student's total performance. This helps to overcome any fears the student and parents may have that the teacher has assessed him or her too early, and that there is little chance for improvement to be recognised.

Individual or group assessments?

The members of any small group are individuals, and establishing a group identity should not result in sacrificing an individual's identity in the classroom. Teachers using the learning framework to organise their lessons will have many opportunities to monitor the contributions and effort of individuals within the small groups, and will be able to take this into account when allocating marks at different stages.

Providing a group mark **may** be appropriate at times - for instance, when students decide that their assessment for a particular product should be for the group as a whole, the teacher may assess on that basis.

However, teachers are often concerned that if a student's work is presented in a version which the whole group has helped to edit and improve, the product will be better than the student could achieve alone. This is precisely the case. Teachers aim to help students improve their work and to do as well as they can. If small group work results in a better product, then it is the result of the work that has gone on in the classroom in order to help the student improve. It is still the achievement of the student in the classroom situation, and the method of instruction does not invalidate the student's achievement. In any case, the teacher who plans for assessment when programming can provide for a variety of methods, so that no student need be continually 'advantaged' in this way.

Requiring students to work toward an excellent finished product, and giving them the opportunity to do this in small groups, also means that they have this experience to draw on when required to work alone.

Where students are able to see the results of their work, to evaluate their success in terms of audience reaction, and to reflect upon the learning process they have experienced, the teacher may find that marks are superfluous. The process, for the learners, has become more important than the product.

Small group work, then, encourages continuous evaluation of the programme designed by the teacher, the work done by students and the learning that occurs. This places the teacher in a position of knowledge about the work of the classroom and the direction to take next. At the same time, students are encouraged to work towards the best kind of learning for them, and towards achieving the best products of the learning experience.

An Afterword: Theory into Practice

We recommend that teachers who are reading this book for the first time should not just accept or reject what is printed here - but **test it** in their classrooms! Whether teachers wish to test a particular strategy only; whether they wish to incorporate into their practice the view of learning described here; or whether they find that the book embraces many of the tacit understandings and methods already used in their classroom practice, *Small Group Learning in the Classroom* may prove helpful in extending and enriching their professional development.

Any systematic classroom investigation is a method of improving teaching practice and therefore student learning. The main aims of undertaking such an investigation (or action research) are to improve specific aspects of practice, and at the same time to deepen understanding of the improvement and its implications, through reflection upon its nature, causes and effects.

The importance of the reflexive nature of this sort of investigation cannot be over-emphasised, and nor can the value of sharing reflection with other teachers engaged in a similar investigation. When selecting a course of systematic classroom investigation, teachers should isolate just what it is that they consider needs investigating and improving, and then use their reflection to enable them to incorporate their findings into future practice.

A simple cycle for systematic classroom investigation, using this book, might consist of these steps.

Isolate those aspects of current practice that are a cause of personal concern.

Plan action over a period of time (possibly during a particular programme of work), and share plans with other teachers for suggestion and comment.

Implement the action as planned.

Observe the action as it occurs in the classroom, noting the effects of the changes made, and the particular circumstances that are in operation at the time.

Reflect upon the action, its effects and the circumstances in which it took place as a rationale for future practice, and share these reflections with other teachers.

If this cycle sounds very much like a regular programming cycle, then a claim that **all** teachers are involved in this type of action, because this is what it means to be professional, can be justified. But the suggestion here that teachers work in conjunction with other teachers to systematically approach changes to their own practice and generalise from that for the future, is very important.

Bibliography

Immensely Practical Books

Judy Clarke, Ron Wideman and Susan Eadie, *Together We Learn.*
  The Metropolitan Toronto School Board, 1988. Prentice-Hall, Scarborough,
  Ontario, 1990.

Joan Dalton, *Adventures in Thinking,* Nelson, Melbourne, 1985.

Alan Howe, *Expanding Horizons: Teaching and Learning through Whole Class
  Discussion.* NATE, Sheffield,1988.

Important Theory

If you only have time to read one book about language and learning theory, choose
one of the following:

Douglas Barnes, *From Communication to Curriculum*, Penguin,
  Harmondsworth, 1976. Available in the United States from Boynton/Cook,
  Portsmouth, New Hampshire.

James Britton, *Language and Learning*, Penguin, Harmondsworth, 1970.
  Available in the United States from Boynton/Cook, Portsmouth, New
  Hampshire.

Margaret Donaldson, *Children's Minds,* London, 1978.

Books produced by Education Departments in Australia

John Carr, *Talking about Talk.* Queensland Education Department, Brisbane,
  1984.

Meredith Maher, *Oral Language in the Secondary School.,* Education
  Department of Victoria, 1983.

Secondary Science Curriculum Committee, *Learning in Science ,* Education
  Department of South Australia, Adelaide, 1979.

Information on the National Oracy Project in the United Kingdom is available
from: The National Oracy Project
      Newcombe House
      45 Notting Hill Gate
      London W11 3JB

Films

As We Talk We Learn. South Australian Film Corporation, 1977. (22 mins)

In a Manner of Speaking. Education Department of Queensland, 1982.
  (in two parts - 19 and 36 mins)

Oracy in Secondary Schools, Wiltshire Oracy Project, 1989.
  (notes and five videos - 10, 24, 22, 15 and 25 mins). Available from Educational
  Video Production, 3 Rokeby Avenue, Bristol BS6 6EJ, England.

Talking to Learn. Education Department of Western Australia, 1979. (29 mins)

Interesting Reading

Douglas Barnes, James Britton and Mike Torbe, *Language, the Learner and the
  School,* (second edition) Penguin, Harmondsworth 1986. Available in the
  United States from Boynton/Cook, Portsmouth, New Hampshire.

Douglas Barnes and Frankie Todd, *Communicating and Learning in Small
  Groups*, Routledge, Kegan Paul, London, 1977.

Tom Brissenden, *Talking about Mathematics: Mathematical Discussion in
  Primary Classrooms*, Blackwell, London, 1988.

Jerome Bruner, *Actual Mind, Possible Worlds*, Cambridge, Massachusetts,
  Harvard University Press, 1986.

Pat Jones, *Lipservice: The Story of Talk in Schools,* Open University Press, Milton
  Keynes, 1988.

Lewis Knowles, *Encouraging Talk*, Methuen, London, 1983.

Jay Lemke, *Using Language in the Classroom*, Deakin University, Geelong, 1985.

Maggie McClure, Terry Phillips and Andrew Wilkinson, *Oracy Matters,* Open
  University Press, Milton Keynes, 1988.

Nancy Martin et al., *Writing and Learning Across the Curriculum 11-16*,
  Ward Lock Education, London, 1976. Available in the United States from
  Boynton/Cook, Portsmouth, New Hampshire.

Mike Torbe and Peter Medway, *The Climate of Learning.* Boynton/Cook,
  Portsmouth, New Hampshire, 1981.